Computer Programming in BASIC

Peter Bishop

Nelson

17064

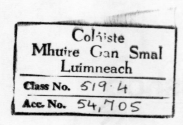
Thomas Nelson and Sons Ltd
Nelson House Mayfield Road
Walton-on-Thames Surrey KT12 5PL

P.O. Box 18123 Nairobi Kenya

116-D JTC Factory Building
Lorong 3 Geylang Square Singapore 1438

Thomas Nelson Australia Pty Ltd
480 La Trobe Street Melbourne Victoria 3000

Nelson Canada Ltd
1120 Birchmount Road Scarborough Ontario M1K 5G4

Thomas Nelson (Hong Kong) Ltd
Watson Estate Block A 13 Floor
Watson Road Causeway Bay Hong Kong

Thomas Nelson (Nigeria) Ltd
8 Ilupeju Bypass PMB 21303 Ikeja Lagos

© Peter Bishop 1978
First published 1978, reprinted 1978, 1980, 1981, 1982 twice

ISBN 0-17-431270-9

NCN 200-3084-5

Design: Phil Kay
Printed in Hong Kong

Introduction

This book is an introduction to BASIC language computer programming, intended mainly for pupils doing an O'level or a CSE in Computer Studies. It caters for pupils of a wide range of interests and abilities, and its use can be varied accordingly.

Three skills are taught:

● Understanding a problem and working out a way of solving it.

● Expressing the method of solution as a flow diagram comprising logically connected steps.

● Translating these steps into a BASIC language computer program.

The language is introduced in gradual stages. Each section of the book introduces a new statement, or a new technique using existing statements. There is at least one worked example, with a description of the method, a flow diagram, the program and the computer printout of the results. Then follows an exercise giving pupils practice in the technique introduced in the section.

Sections marked □ contain material of above average difficulty. They may be omitted without loss of continuity.

The examples and exercises cover a wide range of problems. The emphasis is on actual applications of computers, particularly information processing. In most problems, the mathematical content is minimal. Any formulae which are required are usually supplied in the question.

It is intended that program problems be selected from the exercises, according to the ability and interests of the pupils. There are over 200 program questions in the book. Questions marked □ are of above average difficulty.

At the end of each chapter are exercises of a more general nature, including questions from past examination papers. At the end of the book is a series of longer problems which may form the basis of the projects required by most examination boards, or provide the inevitable computer enthusiasts with some substantial problems of a useful nature to work on.

It is assumed that pupils will be able to run their programs on a microcomputer or a terminal, or use a batch postal system. A chapter is included for programs especially suited for running on terminals or microcomputers.

Unfortunately there are small variations in BASIC language according to the computer and operating system used. All the program examples in this book have been run on the Ipswich Civic College ICL 1900, using a JBAS Mark 2 operating system, or on the Norwich City College ICL 1900, using the Maximop system. Care has been taken to avoid any dubious aspects of the language, but the ultimate test of any program is that it works.

I am grateful to my colleague, Mr. Jeffrey Lake, for the information on which the questions on climatic classification and industrial siting are based.

Contents

1. The first steps

Programming is telling a computer how to perform a task. In order to do this, the task must be split into steps. The instructions for each step must be written in a way that can be interpreted by the computer. This means that the person programming the computer must know precisely how to perform the task himself, even though it might take him a long time.

The words expressing the instructions make up the programming language. The language introduced here, called BASIC (Beginners' All-purpose Symbolic Instruction Code), uses English words and mathematical expressions similar to ordinary algebra. Each instruction is called a *statement*.

Section 1A
Storing information

The main functions of a computer are to store information and to process it. Stored information must be transferred onto the computer (usually from the keyboard of the computer, or from punched cards or paper tape). This is called an *input* process, and the BASIC language instruction for it contains the word READ.

When stored information is required from the computer, it is usually printed on a line printer. This is called an *output* process, and the BASIC language instruction for it contains the word PRINT.

Each item of information is referred to by a letter, called a *variable*. Information, sometimes called *data*, is of two types:

● numbers referred to by (capital) letters, e.g. *A*.

● words, each referred to by a letter followed by a dollar sign, e.g. N$.

Example 1A1

Store on a computer a person's name and telephone number. Print this information.

Method

There are two steps to this problem:

● reading the information onto the computer

● printing it.

Flow diagram

A flow diagram is first drawn. Note the shapes of the boxes, the shape of the middle two being for input or output of information.

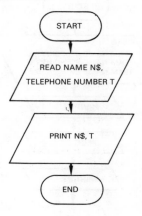

Variables

N$: name   *T*: telephone number

Program

Each step of the problem is written as a statement in BASIC language.

```
 5 READ N$,T
10 PRINT N$,T
15 STOP
20 DATA "STEVEN MARKHAM",4772
25 END
*
```

Results

```
STEVEN MARKHAM    4772
```

Points to notice

● Only capital letters are used.

● Each statement begins with a *line number*. The computer carries out the instructions in order of line number. These usually go up in fives so that lines left out can be easily filled in later.

● Line 20 supplies the information (or data) for the READ statement. For each variable in the READ statement there must be one item in the DATA statement. Words are in inverted commas, numbers are not. Variables are read from the data in order.

● Two statements are needed to finish the program: STOP before the data and END at the end.

Example 1A2

Read the names of three football teams and the number of points they have in the Football League. Print a table of this information.

Method

The steps are the same as before, except there is more information.

Flow diagram

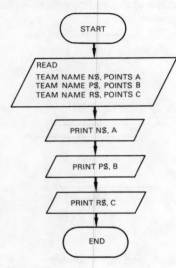

Variables

N$: first team name   A: first team's points
P$: second team name   B: second team's points
R$: third team name   C: third team's points

Program

```
 5 READ N$,A,P$,B,R$,C
10 PRINT N$,A
15 PRINT P$,B
20 PRINT R$,C
25 STOP
30 DATA "LIVERPOOL",46
35 DATA "LEEDS",51
40 DATA "DERBY",29
45 END
*
```

Results

```
LIVERPOOL      46
LEEDS          51
DERBY          29
```

Points to notice

● There can be more than one DATA statement, provided that there is one data item for each variable in the READ statement. (There can also be more than one READ statement.)

● Each PRINT statement starts a new line on the line printer.

● There must be commas between variables or data items in READ, PRINT and DATA statements. There must be no commas at the end of these statements.

Exercise 1A

Copy the flow diagrams and programs for these problems, filling in the missing parts:

1. Read your name and address (three lines) onto the computer, and print an address label.

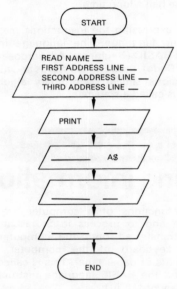

Variables

N$: name   A$: first address line
B$: second address line   C$: third address line

```
 5  READ N$, _____, _____, _____
10  PRINT _____
15  _____ A$
20  _____
25  _____
30  STOP
35  DATA "_____"
40  DATA "_____"
45  _____ " _____ "
50  _____
55  END
```

2. Read the name of a book, its author, date of publication and price. Print this information

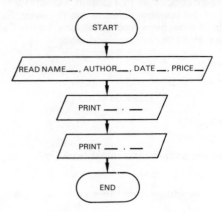

Variables
N$: Name of book   A$: author
D: publication date   P: price

```
 5   READ _____, _____, _____, _____
10   _____ N$, A$
15   PRINT _____, _____
20   STOP
25   _____   "_____",  "_____",
                          _____, _____
30   _____
```

● Note that the price must not have a £ sign.

Draw flow diagrams and write programs for some of these problems. Supply your own data where necessary.

3. Store on the computer the names and prices of four cars. Print this information.

4. Make a list of the names and dates of birth of three people. The data for one person would look like this:

40 DATA "ANN STEVENS", "21/03/62"

The date of birth is in inverted commas as it is not a proper number.

Read this information onto the computer and print a table of it.

5. The amount of money a person has in the bank is called the balance of that person's account. Each account also has an account number. The data with this information for one account is, for example:

50 DATA 416927, "K. R. JACOBSEN", 432·17

Make five similar sets of data, read the information onto the computer and print a table of it.

6. Read, as separate variables, the words: OUTNUMBERED, OUR, THE, ARMY, POWERFUL, DEFEATED, ENEMY. Print several sentences using some or all of the words in different arrangements. Use a new PRINT statement for each sentence.

7. Rewrite the program for this problem, correcting all the mistakes. Remember that a computer will not do a program if there are mistakes in it.

Read the names and population (millions of people) of each of three countries. Print a table of this information.

Variables
A$, B$, C$: names of the countries
P, Q, R: their populations

```
 5   READ A, P, B, Q, C, R
10   PRINT A$, P
15   PRINT B$, Q
25   PRINT C$, R
25   STOP
30   DATA USA, 210·4
35   DATA JAPAN, 108·4
40   DATA, "USSR", 249·8
45   THE END
```

Section 1B
Calculations

Once numbers have been stored on a computer, they can be used in calculations. The BASIC instruction for a calculation uses the word LET.

The calculation is expressed as a formula, very similar to ordinary algebra.

Example 1B1

Read the length and breadth of a rectangle. Calculate and print its area.

Formula
$A = L \times B$
A: area B: breadth L: length

Method
The task has three stages:

● read the length and the breadth

● calculate the area

● print the area

Flow diagram

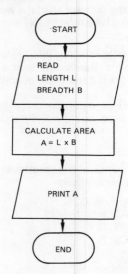

Variables

L: length B: breadth A: area

The calculation step is in a rectangular box.

Program

```
5 READ L,B
10 LET A=L*B
15 PRINT A
20 STOP
25 DATA 16,35
30 END
*
```

Results

```
560
```

Points to notice

The LET statement contains:

- the variable being calculated (here the area A), followed by an equals sign.

- the expression for the calculation, containing other variables or numbers.

- The operations are:

	algebra	BASIC
add	+	+
subtract	−	−
multiply	×	*
divide	÷	/
or fraction	$\dfrac{A}{B}$	A/B

- The order of working is:
  - multiplication and division first
  - addition and subtraction afterwards

Example 1B2

The rate on properties in a certain district is 27p in the pound of the rateable value of the property. Read the address of a property and its rateable value. Calculate the rates. Print the address and rates.

Formula

$R = \cdot 27 \times V$

R: rates (£) V: rateable value (£)

Method

The stages are:

- read the address and rateable value
- calculate the rates
- print the address and rates

Flow diagram

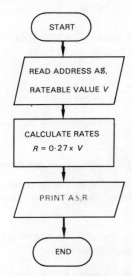

Variables

A$: address R: rates (£)
V: rateable value (£)

Program

```
5 READ A$,V
10 LET R=.27*V
15 PRINT A$,R
20 STOP
25 DATA "117 NORTHFIELD AVENUE",1467.00
30 END
*
```

Results

```
117 NORTHFIELD AVENUE        396.09
```

Points to notice
● There is no £ sign on the rateable value in the DATA statement.

Exercise 1B

Write LET statements for these formulae:

Examples
$E=3A-2$ becomes
LET E=3*A-2

Note: In algebra the multiplication sign is often left out. In BASIC it must always be put in. Thus

$X=\dfrac{YZ}{4}$ becomes

LET X=Y*Z/4

Questions

1. $C=5B$

2. $K=10-3L$

3. $M=\dfrac{P\times Q}{R}$

4. $H=\cdot 37\times J$

5. $S=10-\dfrac{T}{5}$

6. $G=ABC$

7. $X=3Y+2Z$

8. $W=\dfrac{\cdot 4}{X}-\dfrac{\cdot 7}{Y}$

9. $J=3+5H-2K$

10. $C=1\cdot 712D-1\cdot 119E$

Fill in the values of the variables next to each line of the programs:

Example

	P	Q	R	S	T
5 READ P, Q, R	6	4	12	—	—
10 LET S=P+Q	6	4	12	10	—
15 LET T=5*Q−R	6	4	12	10	8
20 PRINT S, T	6	4	12	10	8
25 STOP					
30 DATA 6, 4, 12					
35 END					

Questions

11.
```
 5  READ A, B, C
10  LET D=B−A
15  LET E=B*C+A
20  PRINT D, E
25  STOP
30  DATA 7, 9, 5
35  END
```
A   B   C   D   E

12.
```
 5  READ X, Y
10  LET Z=25−X
15  LET U=X+2*Y−5
20  PRINT U, Z
25  STOP
30  DATA 13, 9
35  END
```
X   Y   Z   U

13.
```
 5  LET K=5
10  READ L, M
15  LET L=L+M
20  LET N=M/5
25  PRINT L, N
30  STOP
35  DATA 4, 15
40  END
```
K   L   M   N

Note: The value of L changes in this program.

Copy these programs, completing the missing parts:

14. Read three numbers and calculate their average. Print the average.

Formulae
$T=A+B+C$
$M=\dfrac{T}{3}$
T: total
A, B, C: numbers   M: average

```
 5  READ _____, _____, _____
10  LET T=_____
15  _____
20  PRINT _____
25  STOP
30  _____
35  END
```

15. Read the name of an article and its price. Calculate the discount on this price at 15%, and the price less discount. Print the name, price, discount and price less discount.

Formulae

$D = \cdot 15 \times P$
$N = P - D$

D: discount (£) P: price (£)
N: price less discount $A\$$: name

```
 5  READ A$, _____
10  LET D=_____
15  LET _____
20  PRINT ____, ____, ____, ____
25  _____
30  DATA "POWER DRILL", 14·20
35  _____
```

Draw flow diagrams and write programs for some of these problems. Supply suitable data where necessary.

16. Cement is sold at 93p per bag. Read an order number and quantity ordered. Calculate the cost. Print the order number, quantity and cost.

Formula

$C = \cdot 93 \times N$

R: order number C: cost (£)
N: quantity ordered

17. Read a length in inches and convert it to millimetres. Print the number of millimetres (1 inch = 25.4 millimetres).

18. The profit of a company is taxed at 40%. Read the name of a company and its profit. Calculate the tax and the amount left (the profit after tax). Print all the information.

Formulae

$T = \cdot 40 \times P$
$N = P - T$

T: tax (£) P: profit (£)
N: profit after tax (£)

19. A lorry carries 1132 kg of sand. Read the name of a month and the number of loads it has carried that month. Calculate the number of kilograms it has carried. Print the month, the number of loads and the number of kilograms.

Formula

$K = 1132 \times L$

K: kilograms L: loads

20. A salesman is paid 20% commission on his sales. For each sale he records the invoice number and the amount. Read this information for three sales

and print a table of it. Add up the amounts, print the total, and calculate and print his commission.

Formulae

$T = A + B + C$
$D = \cdot 20 \times T$

A, B, C: amounts T: total
D: commission

Section 1C
More about LET statements

(This section is more suited to pupils of above average mathematical ability. It may be omitted without causing problems later.)

A more complete list of the operations in BASIC language is:

Operation	Algebra	BASIC
add	+	+
subtract	−	−
multiply	×	*
divide	÷	/
or fraction,		
e.g.:	$\frac{1}{4}$	1/4
brackets	( )	( )
		brackets within brackets are permitted

powers and roots
e.g.: x^2 $\times \uparrow 2$
          $\sqrt{x} = x^{\frac{1}{2}}$ $\times \uparrow (1/2)$

The computer does these in the following order:

1. powers or roots
2. multiplication or division
3. addition or subtraction
4. any calculations in brackets done first of all, again in the above order inside the brackets.

It is better to write powers as repeated multiplications if possible, as this way is quicker to work out.

For example a^2 is better written as A*A
          y^3 as Y*Y*Y

Exercise 1C

Write these formulae as LET statements. Calculate the left hand variable if $A = 1$, $B = 3$, $C = 5$, $X = 0$, $Y = 4$.

Examples

Note carefully the order of calculations.

1. $D=5+2B$

   BASIC: LET $D=5+2*B$
   Calculations:
   $D=5+2\times3$
   $D=5+6$
   $D=11$

2. $E=\dfrac{3A}{5B}$

   BASIC: LET $E=(3*A)/(5*B)$
   Calculations:
   $E=(3\times1)\div(5\times3)$
   $E=3\div15$
   $E=0\cdot2$

3. $F=2C^2+5$

   BASIC: LET $F=2*C*C+5$
   Calculations:
   $F=2\times5\times5+5$
   $F=50+5$
   $F=55$

4. $G=(A+3)^2$

   BASIC: LET $G=(A+3)\uparrow2$
   Calculations:
   $G=(1+3)^2$
   $G=4^2$
   $G=16$

Questions

1. $D=B+3C$

2. $W=5(X+Y)$

3. $U=Y^2-2X$

4. $V=\dfrac{4}{3}\times3\cdot14159\times R^3$

5. $C=\dfrac{A}{Y}+\dfrac{B}{Y}$

6. $D=\dfrac{A+B}{2C}$

7. $E=\dfrac{A}{2C}$

8. $J=\dfrac{12}{A+2}$

9. $Z=3X+4Y$

10. $K=(AC)^B$

Section 1D
Headings

Up to now, only information read or calculated has been printed. Headings, units or other information can be printed by putting it in inverted commas in PRINT statements.

Example 1D1

Interest is paid on a sum of money if it is saved in a bank or building society for a time. The formula is

$$I=\dfrac{PRT}{100}$$

P: sum of money (£) R: interest rate (%)
T: time saved (years) I: interest (£)

Read a sum of money, interest rate and time, calculate the interest and print all the information with suitable headings and units.

Flow diagram

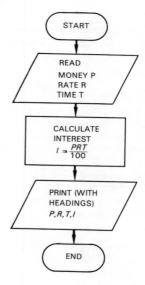

Program

```
 5 READ P,R,T
10 LET I=P*R*T/100
15 PRINT "SUM OF MONEY:","£";P
20 PRINT "INTEREST RATE:",R;"%"
25 PRINT "TIME:",T;"YEARS"
30 PRINT "INTEREST:", "£";I
35 STOP
40 DATA 37.25,8,13
45 END
*
```

7

Results

```
SUM OF MONEY:  £ 37.25
INTEREST RATE:  8 %
TIME:          13 YEARS
INTEREST:      £ 38.74
```

Points to notice

● The semicolon in the PRINT statement causes a closer spacing of the items printed. Semicolons must not be used in READ or DATA statements.

● No units are included in the DATA statement. The three numbers represent £37·25, 8% and 13 years.

Example 1D2

At a factory producing machine parts, the production rate is 37 parts per hour. An order has the following information:

order number, customer's name, quantity

Read this information, calculate the production time and print all the information under suitable headings.

Formula

$$T = \frac{N}{37}$$

T: production time (hours) N: number of parts
R: order number C: customer's name

Flow diagram

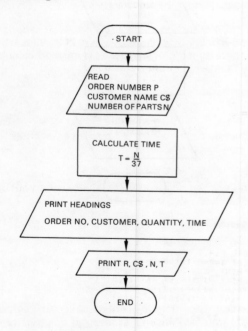

Program

```
5 READ R,C$,N
10 LET T=N/37
15 PRINT "ORDER NO.","CUSTOMER","QUANTITY","TIME(HRS)"
20 PRINT R,C$,N,T
25 STOP
30 DATA 4633,"A.F.ADAMSON",2750
35 END
```

Results

ORDER NO.	CUSTOMER	QUANTITY	TIME(HRS)
4633	A.F.ADAMSON	2750	74.3243

Points to notice

● The variables in line 20 must be in the same order as the headings in line 15.

Exercise 1D

Copy the programs for these problems, filling in the missing parts.

1. A sum of money is to be divided amongst a number of people. Read the amount of money and the number of people, and calculate how much each gets. Print all the information, suitably labelled.

Formula

$$S = \frac{A}{N}$$

S: share (£) A: sum of money
N: number of people

```
 5 READ ____, ____
10 PRINT "SUM OF MONEY", "£"; ____
15 PRINT "NUMBER OF PEOPLE" ____
20 LET ____ = ____
25 PRINT "SHARE", "____"; S
30 STOP
35 DATA 1486·64, 8
40 ____
```

2. Read the number of tons that an oil tanker can carry (variable N), and the number of voyages it makes in a year (variable V). Calculate the number of tons it carries in that year (variable T).

Formula

$$T = N \times V$$

```
 5 READ N, V
10 PRINT "TONS CARRIED", ____
15 PRINT "_____"; ____
20 LET _____ = _____
25 PRINT _____
30 STOP
35 DATA _____, _____
40 END
```

3. A chemical is supplied in 25 kg and 50 kg bags. Read the number of 25 kg bags (variable R) and the number of 50 kg bags (variable S) making up an

8

order. Calculate the weight of each type (variables L and P) and the total weight (variable T). Print all the information, suitably labelled.

```
 5 READ R, S
10 LET L=25*____
15 LET P=_____
20 LET T=_____+_____
25 PRINT "WEIGHT OF 25 KG BAGS", ____;
                                      "KG"
30 PRINT "_____", P; "KG"
35 PRINT "_____",
              _____; "_____"
40 STOP
45 DATA _____, _____
50 END
```

Draw flow diagrams and write programs for some of these problems. Print all the information read or calculated in the problems, with suitable headings and units. Supply your own data where necessary.

4. The average number of hours that people spent watching television per week was 18·9 in February 1972, and 19·7 in February 1975. Read these figures and calculate the percentage increase.

Formula

$$P=\frac{(B-A)\times100}{A}$$

B: 1975 figure A: 1972 figure
P: percentage increase

5. Read the name of an article you would like to buy, its price, and the amount you can save per week. Calculate the number of weeks it would take to save up for it.

Formula

$$W=\frac{P}{S}$$

W: number of weeks P: price (£)
S: weekly savings (£) $N\$$: name of article

6. Read the name of an article, its price and VAT rate (which is 15 per cent at present). Calculate the VAT and price plus VAT. Print the name, price, VAT and price plus VAT.

Formulae

$$V=\frac{P\times R}{100}$$
$$T=V+P$$

V: VAT (£) P: price (£) R: VAT rate (%)
T: price+VAT

7. At a warehouse, the following information is punched on a data card for each item stored, each week:

	Variable
item number	N
name	$A\$$
number in stock the previous week	P
number added during the week	L
number removed during the week	R

Read this information and calculate the number currently in stock.

Formula

$C=P+L-R$

C: current number in stock

8.

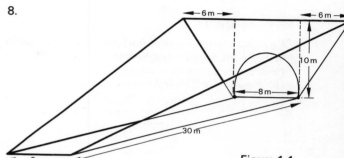

Figure 1.1

Calculate the volume of earth that must be removed to dig the entrance to the railway tunnel shown in Figure 1.1. Work out the formulae yourself. No extra lengths need to be calculated.

9. In 1974 there were 3 723 743 pupils at secondary school in England and Wales, and 202 298 teachers in these schools. Read these figures and calculate the number of pupils per teacher.

Formula

$$R=\frac{P}{T}$$

P: number of pupils R: pupils per teacher
T: number of teachers

Modification

Find out the corresponding numbers for your own school and use them instead.

Note: Long program statements have sometimes had to be split into two lines to fit into the columns of the book. This applies to statements 25 and 35 of the program in question 3.

When programs are written, each statement must occupy one line only.

Section 1E
Remarks

Information identifying a program, explaining how it works, or giving the meanings of the variables, can be supplied by REMARK statements (usually shortened to REM). These statements may be placed anywhere in the program, and are not acted on by the computer in any way.

Example 1E1

Calculate the total area of the walls of a room, reading in its length, breadth and height.
(wall area = perimeter × height)
i.e. $W = 2 \times (L + B) \times H$

Flow diagram

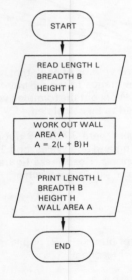

Variables

L: length (ft)	B: breadth (ft)
H: height (ft)	W: wall area (ft²)

Program

```
5 REM PROGRAM TO CALCULATE TOTAL WALL AREA
10 READ L,B,H
15 REM L:LENGTH (FT),B:BREADTH (FT),H:HEIGHT (FT)
20 LET W=2*H*(L+B)
25 REM W:WALL AREA (FT↑2)
30 PRINT "LENGTH:",L;"FT"
35 PRINT "BREADTH:",B;"FT"
40 PRINT "HEIGHT:",H;"FT"
45 PRINT "WALL AREA:",W;"FT↑2"
50 STOP
55 REM DATA CAN BE VARIED FOR DIFFERENT ROOMS
60 DATA 11,8,7.5
65 END
*
```

Results

```
LENGTH:          11 FT
BREADTH:         8 FT
HEIGHT:          7.5 FT
WALL AREA:       285 FT↑2
```

Points to notice

● The word REM can be followed by letters, numbers or punctuation marks. Inverted commas are not necessary.

Include remark statements in your programs wherever you feel they are appropriate.

Exercise 1E

This exercise covers the various topics introduced in this chapter.

Copy the programs for these problems, filling in the missing parts:

1. Read the names and heights (centimetres) of three people. Print a list of this information.

    ### Variables
    N\$, M\$, P\$: names
    H, I, J: heights (cm)

    ```
     5 READ N$, H, M$, ____, ____, ____
    10 PRINT N$, ____
    15 PRINT ____, I
    20 _____
    25 STOP
    30 DATA "_____", ____
    35 DATA _____
    40 _____
    45 END
    ```

2. Read a temperature in degrees Centigrade and convert it to degrees Fahrenheit.

    ### Formula
    $$F = 32 + \frac{C \times 9}{5}$$

    C: degrees Centigrade F: degrees Fahrenheit

    ```
     5 READ C
    10 LET F=_____
    15 PRINT "_____", C
    20 PRINT _____
    25 _____
    30 DATA ____
    35 END
    ```

Write the following formulae as LET statements. Work out the value of the left hand variable if $D = 2$, $E = 3$, $F = 0$, $G = -2$.

3. $P \Rightarrow 2D + 3E$

4. $R = 2E \div (D + 1)$

5. $S=E+G$

6. $T=DE+EF$

7. $U=4(D^2-G)$

Copy the tables next to the following programs, writing in the values of the variables at each line.

	A	B	C	D	T	M

8. 5 READ A, B, C, D
    10 LET T=A+B+C+D
    15 LET M=T/4
    20 PRINT M
    25 STOP
    30 DATA 3, 5, 7, 1
    35 END

	A	B	C	P	Q	R

9. 5 READ P, Q, R
    10 LET A=P*Q
    15 LET B=3*P−2*R
    20 LET C=P+Q−R
    25 PRINT A, B, C
    30 STOP
    35 DATA 7, 9, 5
    40 END

Draw flow diagrams and write programs for some of the following problems. Supply suitable data.

10. Make a list of the names of the top five records in the hit parade. Write a program to read these names from data cards and print them.

11. Store on the computer the distance from your home to school, and the number of times you make this journey in a year (there are about 190 school days in a year). Calculate the total distance you travel to and from school in a year. Print, with suitable headings and units, the distance to school, number of journeys, and total distance travelled.

Formula
$T=D\times J$

T: total distance D: distance to school
J: number of journeys

12. An aeroplane carries first class and tourist class passengers. For each flight, a data card is prepared with:

	Variable
flight number	N
number of first class passengers	A
first class fare (£)	B
number of tourist class passengers	C
tourist class fare (£)	D

Write a program to read this in information, calculate the total fare, and print all the information with suitable labels.

Formula
$T=A\times B+C\times D$
T: total fare (£)

13. Work out the length of the hypotenuse of a right-angled triangle, reading the lengths of the other two sides. Print all three lengths with headings and units:

Formula
$H=\sqrt{A^2+B^2}$
H: hypotenuse A, B: other sides

☐ 14. Complete the design of the rocket in Figure 1.2 by supplying the lengths D, H, K, F and G.

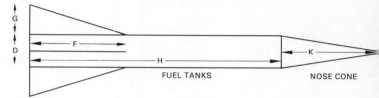

FUEL TANKS   NOSE CONE

Read these lengths and calculate:

overall length: $L=H+K$
fin area: $A=\dfrac{F\times G}{2}$
fuel tank capacity: $C=\dfrac{3\cdot142\times D^2\times H}{4}$
fuel tank surface area: $S=3\cdot142\times D\times H$
nose cone volume: $V=\dfrac{3\cdot142\times D^2\times K}{12}$
nose cone surface area: $R=\dfrac{3\cdot142\times D}{2}\times\sqrt{\left(\dfrac{D^2}{4}+K^2\right)}$

Print all the information with suitable headings and units.

15. Make up other programs using the methods you have learned in this chapter.

16. Rewrite the program for this problem, correcting all the mistakes:

Read a person's name and his weekly wage. Calculate his year's wage by multiplying the weekly wage by 52. Print his name and both wages.

```
 5 READ N, W
10 LET Y=52W
15 PRINT  NAME, WEEKLY WAGE, YEAR'S
                                  WAGE
20 PRINT N. Y. W
25 STOP
30 DATA A. L. HOLDEN, £52.16
30 END
```

17. A telephone bill is worked out for a customer using the information and formulae in the flowchart. The data is input in the form: customer number; dialled units (D).

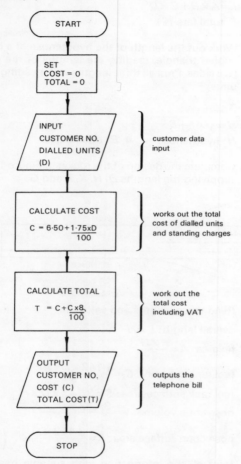

```
          START

          SET
          COST = 0        } 
          TOTAL = 0

          INPUT
          CUSTOMER NO.     } customer data
          DIALLED UNITS      input
          (D)

          CALCULATE COST   } works out the total
                               cost of dialled units
          C = 6·50 + 1·75xD    and standing charges
                    ───────
                      100

          CALCULATE TOTAL  } work out the
                               total cost
          T  = C + C x 8      including VAT
                    ─────
                     100

          OUTPUT
          CUSTOMER NO.     } outputs the
          COST (C)           telephone bill
          TOTAL COST(T)

          STOP
```

Write a program in high-level language to calculate the telephone bill and to output the bill to include customer number; cost (C); total cost (T).

Credit will be given for presentation of output.

(Welsh Joint Education Committee)

☐ 18. For a named high-level language describe arrangements for input and output, including the control of layout.

Write a program to read the dimensions of a rectangular room and calculate and print the area of the ceiling and the volume of the room. Your program should include explanatory comments, and the output should be self-explanatory.

(Oxford Local Examinations)

2. Program loops

A major advantage of computers over previous calculating devices is their ability to perform calculations and other operations repeatedly. A section of a program which is performed repeatedly is called a loop.

Section 2A
Counters

A variable is always used to count the number of times the loop has been performed. This variable is referred to as a counter.

The counter:

● starts at a certain value (usually 1)

● ends at a certain value (usually the number of times the loop is repeated)

● is increased by a certain amount (the step, usually 1) each time the loop is performed.

Example 2A1

Part of a program is to be repeated ten times. Counter K goes from 1 to 10 in steps of 1.

Flow diagram   **Program**

10 FOR K = 1 TO 10 STEP 1

... part of program to be repeated

40 NEXT K

Points to notice

Flow diagram

● The diamond shaped box is for a decision, always in the form of a question. Two arrows always come out of a decision box, one marked YES and the other NO. The decision is whether or not the loop has been repeated ten times.

Program

● A loop always starts with the word FOR. This statement contains:

  ● the loop counter (here K)
  ● the starting value of the counter (here 1)
  ● the final value of the counter (here 10)
  ● the step size (here 1)

● A loop ends with the word NEXT. This statement also contains the loop counter.

● The value of the counter changes while the program is running. In general, any variable can change its value during the running of a program.

● The word STEP may be left out if the step is 1. For example
    FOR K=1 TO 10
means the same as
    FOR K=1 TO 10 STEP 1

Exercise 2A

Draw the parts of the flow diagrams and write FOR and NEXT statements for:

1. A loop to be repeated for counter L from 1 to 8 in steps of 1.

2. A part of a program to be repeated twelve times, using counter A.

3. Part of a program to be repeated for values of B from 0 to 100 in steps of 5. (How many times will this loop be performed?)

4. A loop to be repeated with variable M starting at 1·5 and going up in steps of 0·5 until it reaches 6·5.

5. A loop to be repeated for counter K going from A to B in steps of C. Variables A, B and C are read before the loop starts.

Example 2B1

Read the departure time and destination of six trains from your local station. Print a list of this information.

Method

The part of the program to be repeated is the reading and printing of the information. A counter K is used, running from 1 to 6 in steps of 1.

Flow diagram

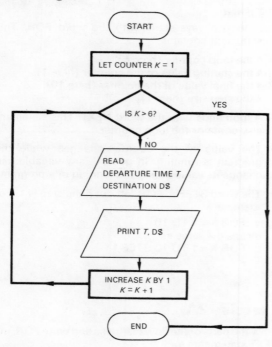

Variables

T: departure time   D$: destination
K: counter

Program

```
5 FOR K=1 TO 6 STEP 1
10 READ T,D$
15 PRINT T,D$
20 NEXT K
25 STOP
30 DATA 0835,"BIRMINGHAM"
35 DATA 0910,"LONDON"
40 DATA 0920,"LIVERPOOL"
45 DATA 0935,"EDINBURGH"
50 DATA 1014,"BRISTOL"
55 DATA 1046,"LONDON"
60 END
*
```

Results

```
0835          BIRMINGHAM
910           LONDON
920           LIVERPOOL
935           EDINBURGH
1014          BRISTOL
1046          LONDON
```

Points to notice

● Although there is only one READ statement, it is carried out six times. There must be six sets of data.

● The loop counter must be different from any letter used inside the loop.

Example 2B2

Each working day at a factory, a record is made of the production of the machines. For each machine, a data card is prepared with the date, machine number, number of items produced and the number of running hours.

Write a program to read eight such data cards and calculate the number of items produced per hour (the production rate) for each machine.

Print a table of the information, with headings

DATE   MACHINE NO.   PRODUCTION HOURS PRODUCTION RATE

Formula

$$R \quad \frac{P}{T}$$

R: production rate P: number of items produced
T: hours running

Method

First the headings are printed.

A loop follows, with counter L from 1 to 8 in steps of 1, in which:

● the information is read from a data card

● the production rate is calculated

● the input information and production rate are printed.

Flow diagram

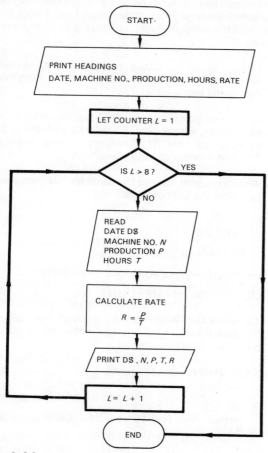

Variables

L: counter   D$: date N: machine number
P: number of items produced T: hours running
R: production rate

Program

```
5 PRINT "DATE","MACHINE NO.","PRODUCTION","HOURS","PRODUCTION RATE"
10 FOR L=1 TO 8 STEP 1
15 READ D$,N,P,T
20 LET R=P/T
25 PRINT D$,N,P,T,R
30 NEXT L
35 STOP
40 DATA "21/03/76",14, 463,17.3
45 DATA "21/03/76", 9,1412,19.5
50 DATA "21/03/76",23, 537,12.2
55 DATA "22/03/76",18,1737,21.6
60 DATA "22/03/76",14, 527,18.4
65 DATA "22/03/76", 5, 981, 8.7
70 DATA "23/03/76", 6,1156,18.3
75 DATA "23/03/76",21, 85, 0.9
80 END
```

Results

DATE	MACHINE NO.	PRODUCTION	HOURS	PRODUCTION RATE
21/03/76	14	463	17.3	26.763
21/03/76	9	1421	19.5	72.8718
21/03/76	23	537	12.2	14.0164
22/03/76	18	1737	21.6	80.4167
22/03/76	14	527	18.4	28.6413
22/03/76	5	981	8.7	112.759
23/03/76	6	1156	18.3	63.1694
23/03/76	21	85	.9	94.4444

Points to notice

● The variables in the PRINT statement in line 25 must be in the same order as the headings in line 5.

● Spaces are left in the DATA statements to line up the numbers in columns. This makes card punching and reading easier.

● The headings must be printed before the loop starts.

Exercise 2B

Copy the flow diagrams and programs for these problems, completing the missing parts:

1. Read the names (variable N$), addresses (variable A$) and telephone numbers (variable T) of four people and print them.

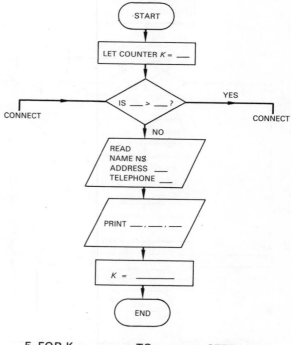

```
 5 FOR K=_____ TO _____ STEP _____
10 READ N$, _____, _____
15 PRINT _____
20 NEXT _____
25 STOP
30 DATA "MR. S. KENNEDY", "41 GRAHAM
                         ROAD, CROYDON", 2137
35 DATA "_____", "_____
                                    _____", _____
40 DATA _____
45 _____
50 END
```

2. Read the mass and volume of five substances and calculate the density of each. Print a table with headings

MASS   VOLUME   DENSITY

Formula

$D = \dfrac{M}{V}$

D: density M: mass V: volume

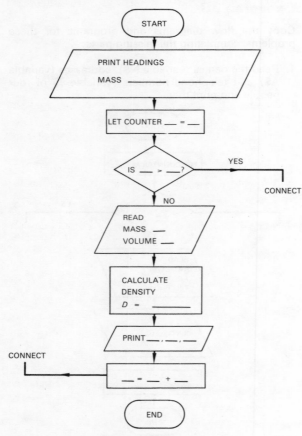

```
 5  PRINT "MASS", "_____", "_____"
10  FOR K=_____
15  READ M, V
20  LET D=_____
15  PRINT _____, _____, _____
20  NEXT K
25  _____
30  DATA 416, 74
35  DATA _____, _____
40  _____
45  _____
50  _____
55  END
```

Write flow diagrams and programs for some of these problems. The counter must be a different variable from any which are read or calculated in the loop. Check that you include enough data, and that it is in the right order.

3. Make a list of the names and prices of six grocery items. Write a program to read this information from data cards and print it.

4. A coal merchant charges £9.54 per ton of coal. For each order, a data card is prepared with the order number (variable R), customer's name (variable C$) and number of tons (variable N).

   Write a program to read the cards for five orders and calculate the cost of each.

   Formula
   $C = 9.54 \times N$
   C: cost (£)

   Print a table of the information headed:

   ORDER NO.   NAME   TONS   COST (£)

5. Calculate the weekly pay for each of ten workers. For each worker, read a works number, name, hourly pay rate and hours worked.

   Calculate pay from the formula

   $P = R \times H$
   P: pay (£)
   R: rate per hour (e.g. 96p per hour is written as $\cdot 96$)
   H: hours

   Print a table of all the information.

6. The four members of a rock group agree on what percentage of their year's income each should get. Read their income (variable L), then use a loop to read the name of each member (variable N$) and his percentage (variable P). The percentages must add up to 100. Calculate the share that each member gets. Print their names, percentages and shares.

   Formula
   $S = \dfrac{P \times L}{100}$
   S: share (£)

7. A shop sells goods on hire purchase on these terms: there is a deposit of 20% of the price, the rest being paid back in equal monthly instalments. For each of ten items, read in the name, price and number of instalments. Calculate the deposit and monthly payment. Print the results in a suitable table.

Formulae

$$D = \cdot20 \times P$$

$$M = \frac{P - D}{N}$$

D: deposit (£) P: price (£)   I$: name
M: monthly payment (£) N: number of instalments

8. The average weekly earnings (£) of workers in the UK from 1970 to 1974 were:

Year	Men	Women
1970	28·05	13·99
1971	30·93	15·80
1972	35·82	18·30
1973	40·92	21·16
1974	48·63	27·01

Read this information from data cards, and calculate the difference between the men's wage and the women's wage each year. Print a table like the one above, with an extra column for the differences.

Formula

$$D = M - W$$

D: difference M: men's wage
W: women's wage

9. The number of cars in EEC countries in 1972 was as follows:

(millions of cars)

Country	Cars (1972)	% increase (1961 to 1972)
UK	13·2	105
Belgium	2·3	172
Denmark	1·2	145
France	13·4	118
West Germany	15·6	202
Ireland	0·4	134
Italy	12·5	409
Luxembourg	0·1	165
Netherlands	2·8	355

Write a program to read this information, and estimate the number of cars in each country in 1983 if the present percentage increase continues.

Formula

$$M = N \times (1 + \frac{P}{100})$$

M: cars in 1983 N: cars in 1972 P: % increase
C$: name of country

Print a table with headings:

ESTIMATES OF CAR NUMBERS (MILLIONS) IN
                                THE EEC
COUNTRY   CARS (1972)   CARS (1983)

Section 2C
Adding up totals in loops

Many problems require the total of a fairly large set of numbers. This is best done in a loop, as the following example shows.

Example 2C1

Calculate the average of 20 numbers.

Method

- The total (variable T) is set to zero before the loop starts.

- Inside the loop, each number (variable N) is read, and added to the total ($T = T + N$).

- After the loop, T is the total of all the numbers. It is divided by 20 to find the average.

Flow diagram

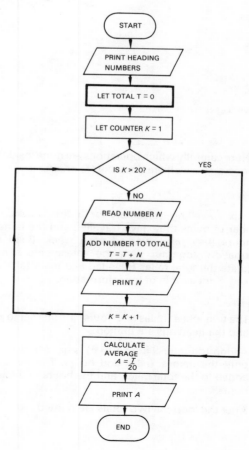

Variables

T: total   *K*: counter
N: numbers   *A*: average

Program

```
5 PRINT "NUMBERS"
10 LET T=0
15 FOR K=1 TO 20 STEP 1
20 READ N
25 LET T=T+N
30 PRINT N
35 NEXT K
40 LET A=T/20
45 PRINT "AVERAGE:",A
50 STOP
55 DATA 7,5,3,11,15,1,27,2,9,8,14,6,7,9,8,4,2,1,9,3
60 END
*
```

Results

```
NUMBERS
 7
 5
 3
 11
 15
 1
 27
 2
 9
 8
 14
 6
 7
 9
 8
 4
 2
 1
 9
 3
AVERAGE:      7.55
```

Points to notice

● Note carefully which operations are done inside the loop and which are done before or after it.

Example 2C2

The six travelling salesmen for a firm record the number of miles they have travelled and the number of hours they have worked each week. Read this information, together with the salesmen's names. Calculate the total miles travelled and the total hours worked. Print a table of the information.

Method

● The two totals (miles and hours) are first set to zero and the headings are printed.

● A loop (counter *S* from 1 to 6) is used to read and print the names, miles and hours. The miles are added to the total miles, and the hours to the total hours.

● After the loop the two totals are printed.

Flow diagram

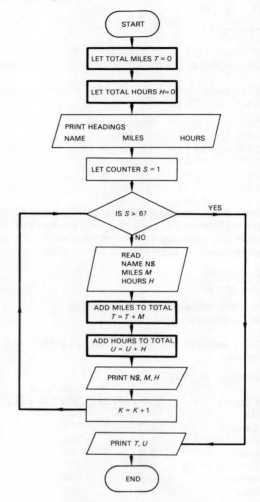

Variables

N$: name   *M*: miles   *H*: hours   *T*: total miles
U: total hours   *S*: counter

Program

```
5 LET T=0
10 LET U=0
15 PRINT "NAME","MILES","HOURS"
20 FOR S=1 TO 6 STEP 1
25 READ N$,M,H
30 LET T=T+M
35 LET U=U+H
40 PRINT N$,M,H
45 NEXT S
50 PRINT "TOTALS",T,U
55 STOP
60 DATA "R.J.PATERSON",437,42
65 DATA "M.HUMPHRIES",521,33
70 DATA "K.JACOBS"    ,719,37
75 DATA "M.D.WALTERS",371,39
80 DATA "A.DAVIDSON"  ,817,43
85 DATA "J.ADAMS"     ,418,37
90 END
*
```

Results

NAME	MILES	HOURS
R.J.PATERSON	437	42
M.HUMPHRIES	521	33
K.JACOBS	719	37
M.D.WALTERS	371	39
A.DAVIDSON	817	43
J.ADAMS	418	37
TOTALS	3283	231

Exercise 2C

1. Copy and complete the flow diagram and program for this problem.

   The costs of building a new house were:

site	£4500
materials	£3124
labour	£2941
architect	£895
legal fees	£319
other	£247

   Read and print the name of each item (N$) and its cost (C). Calculate and print the total cost (T).

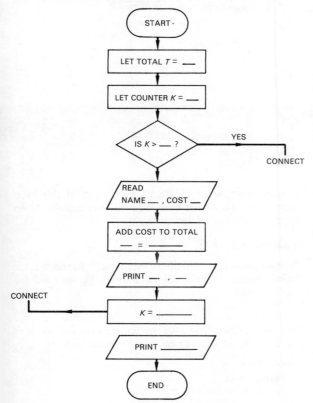

```
 5  LET T=_____
10  FOR K=_____ TO _____ STEP _____
15  READ N$, _____
20  LET T=_____
25  PRINT _____
30  _____
35  PRINT "_____",  _____
40  STOP
45  DATA "SITE", 4500
50  DATA "_____", _____
55  DATA _____
60  DATA _____
65  DATA _____
70  DATA _____
75  END
```

Draw flow diagrams and write programs for some of these problems:

2. A shipping line has five cargo ships. The number of tons transported by each ship in a three-month period was:

M.V. Newhaven	42321
M.V. Plymouth	38416
M.V. Penzance	29117
M.V. Alberta	33220
M.V. Ontario	19317

   Read this information and print it. Calculate and print the total number of tons transported.

3. Calculate the average of 10 numbers.

4. A school orders eight different types of textbook from a bookseller. Read in the reference number, quantity and price for each type. Calculate the cost (cost=quantity × price) and the total cost. Print an invoice with columns headed:

   REFERENCE NUMBER   QUANTITY   PRICE   COST

   Print the total cost underneath.

☐ 5. Write a program to read in a bank account number, the amount in the account (the balance), and then ten deposits or withdrawals, each with a date. Withdrawals are entered as negative numbers, so both are added to the balance to get the new balance (the data for a withdrawal of £13·47 on 17th February 1976 would be: 170276, −13·47). A bank statement is printed, showing the account number and original balance, and then columns for the date, deposit or withdrawal, and new balance.

6. Each section of a railway line can be taken at a certain speed, depending on the gradient, curvature, etc. Read in the distance and speed of eight sections of a line. Calculate the time to cover each section, and the total distance and time for the line. Also calculate the average speed. Print a suitable table of the various quantities.

$T = D \div S$

T: time (hours) D: distance (miles)
S: speed (mph)

$A = T1 \div T2$

A: average speed $T1$: total distance
$T2$: total time

7. On a cable-laying ship, a daily record is kept of the number of hours worked and the number of metres of cable laid. Write a program to read in this information for 10 days, calculate the total working time, total length of cable laid, and the average number of metres laid per hour.

$A = L \div T$

A: average metres laid per hour
L: total number of metres laid
T: total number of working hours

8. A survey was made to find out the average age of the cars passing a certain place. The number of cars of each age (in years) was:

Age	Number of cars	Age	Number of cars	Age	Number of cars
0	9	4	19	8	3
1	22	5	22	9	0
2	35	6	17	10	1
3	28	7	9	11	0

Write a program to read these results (or preferably similar ones of your own) and calculate the average age:

● Set total age and total cars to zero.

● Use a loop to read and print the information. Add the number of cars to the total cars. Multiply the number of cars by the age and add the answer to the total age.

● After the loop, calculate the average age:

$$\text{average} = \frac{\text{total age}}{\text{total cars}}$$

9. The table shows the populations and areas of the EEC countries. Write a program to read this information from data cards, and calculate the number of people per square kilometre (the population density) in each country.

Formula

$$D = \frac{P \times 1000}{A}$$

P: population (millions of people)
D: population density
A: area (thousands of square kilometres)

Country	Population (millions)	Area (thousands of square kilometres)
UK	55·93	244·0
Belgium	9·76	30·5
Denmark	5·03	43·1
France	52·13	547·0
West Germany	61·97	248·6
Irish Republic	3·03	70·3
Italy	54·89	301·2
Luxembourg	0·35	2·6
Netherlands	13·44	40·8

Print a table with suitable headings.

Modification

Add up the total population and total area. Calculate the average population density.

Formula

$$E = \frac{T \times 1000}{U}$$

T: total population (millions)
U: total area (thousands of square kilometres)
E: average population density

Section 2D
Tables

A large number of problems make use of the loop counter in the actual calculations, particularly when producing tables of various kinds.

Example 2D1

Print a conversion table from inches to centimetres, for inches from 1 inch to 12 inches (1 inch = 2·54 centimetres).

Method

The loop counter I is also the variable for inches. It is used inside the loop to calculate the centimetres:

$C = 2·54 \times I$
C: centimetres

The values of C and I are printed.

Flow diagram

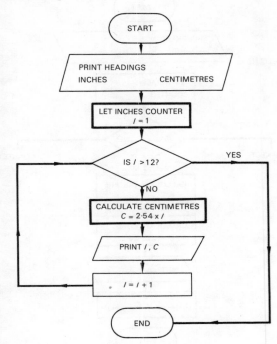

Variables

I: counter (inches)   *C*: centimetres

Program

```
5 PRINT "INCHES","CENTIMETRES"
10 FOR I=1 TO 12 STEP 1
15 LET C=2.54*I
20 PRINT I,C
25 NEXT I
30 STOP
35 END
*
```

Results

INCHES	CENTIMETRES
1	2.54
2	5.08
3	7.62
4	10.16
5	12.7
6	15.24
7	17.78
8	20.32
9	22.86
10	25.4
11	27.94
12	30.48

Points to notice

● There are no READ or DATA statements.

● The loop counter is used in the calculations.

Example 2D2

Print a table of the VAT to be paid on prices from 5p to £1·00 in intervals of 5p, and the price plus VAT.

Formulae

$$V=\frac{P\times R}{100}$$
$$T=P+V$$

V: VAT (p)   *P*: price (p)   *T*: price+VAT (p)
R: VAT rate (%)

Method

● The rate *R* is read and the headings printed.

● A loop is made, with counter *P* (price) going from 5 to 100 in steps of 5. Inside the loop, variables *V* and *T* are calculated. *P*, *V* and *T* are printed.

Flow diagram

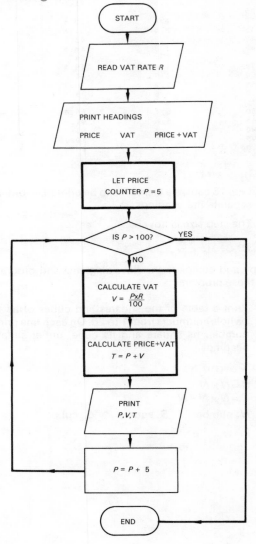

Program

```
5 READ R
10 PRINT "V.A.T. TABLE AT";R;"%"
15 PRINT
20 PRINT "PRICE","V.A.T.","PRICE + V.A.T."
25 FOR P= 5 TO 100 STEP 5
30 LET V=P*R/100
35 LET T=V+P
40 PRINT P,V,T
45 NEXT P
45 NEXT P
50 STOP
55 DATA 8
60 END
*
```

Results

PRICE	V.A.T.	PRICE + V.A.T.
5	.4	5.4
10	.8	10.8
15	1.2	16.2
20	1.6	21.6
25	2	27
30	2.4	32.4
35	2.8	37.8
40	3.2	43.2
45	3.6	48.6
50	4	54
55	4.4	59.4
60	4.8	64.8
65	5.2	70.2
70	5.6	75.6
75	6	81
80	6.4	86.4
85	6.8	91.8
90	7.2	97.2
95	7.6	102.6
100	8	108

Points to notice

● Line 15 causes a blank line to be printed, in order to separate the headings.

● The step size is now 5.

Exercise 2D

Copy and complete the flow diagrams and programs for these problems:

1. Print a table of the squares and cubes of all the (whole) numbers from 1 to 20. On each line print a number, its square and its cube, under suitable headings.

   ### Formulae

   $S = N \times N$
   $C = N \times N \times N$

   N: number S: square C: cube

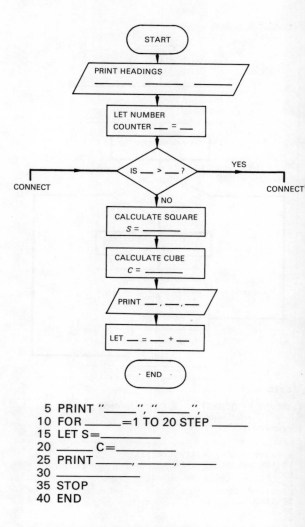

```
 5  PRINT "_____", "_____",
10  FOR _____=1 TO 20 STEP _____
15  LET S=_____
20  _____ C=_____
25  PRINT _____, _____, _____
30  _____
35  STOP
40  END
```

2. When an object is dropped, it falls under the influence of gravity, accelerating all the time. The distance it has fallen is calculated from:

   $D = 4 \cdot 9 \times T^2$

   D: distance fallen (metres)
   T: time taken (seconds)

   Print a table of distances fallen for times up to 25 seconds.

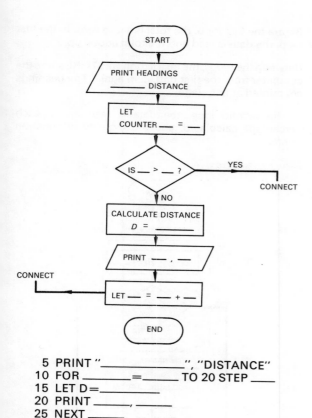

```
START

PRINT HEADINGS
_____ DISTANCE

LET
COUNTER ___ = ___

IS ___ > ___ ?        YES
                            CONNECT
         NO

CALCULATE DISTANCE
D = _____

PRINT ___ , ___

CONNECT
         LET ___ = ___ + ___

END
```

```
 5 PRINT "_____", "DISTANCE"
10 FOR _____ = _____ TO 20 STEP ____
15 LET D=_____
20 PRINT _____ , _____
25 NEXT _____
30 STOP
35 END
```

Draw flow diagrams and write programs for some of these problems. In most questions READ and DATA statements are not required. The loop counters are used in the actual calculations.

3. Print a table of the square roots of the numbers from 1 to 25.

   Formula

   $R=N^{.5}$

   R: square root N: number (loop counter)

4. Print a table of the reciprocals of the numbers from 1 to 20.

   Formula

   $S=\dfrac{1}{N}$

   S: reciprocal N: number

5. Print a conversion table from kilograms to pounds, from 1 kilogram to 20 kilograms.

   Formula

   $P=2\cdot2\times K$

   P: pounds K: kilograms

6. Print a conversion table from pounds to grams, from 1 pound to 25 pounds.

   Formula

   $G=453\cdot6\times P$

   G: grams P: pounds

7. Print a table of volumes of spheres of radii 1 centimetre to 10 centimetres at 1 centimetre intervals. On each line print a radius and the corresponding volume.

   Formula

   $V=\dfrac{4\times3\cdot142\times R^3}{3}$

   V: volume R: radius

8. Print a table of the sizes of the interior angles of regular polygons, with the number of sides ranging from 3 to 30.

   Formula

   $A=180-\dfrac{360}{N}$

   N: number of sides A: interior angle

9. A sum of money is invested at a certain rate of compound interest. Every year, interest is added to the sum, the formula for the total amount being:

   $A=P\times(1+\dfrac{R}{100})^T$

   A: amount (£) P: sum of money (£)
   R: interest rate (%) T: time (years)

   Read from data the sum of money and the interest rate. Print a table of amounts over times from 1 to 20 years.

10. Print a table of the times taken to travel a certain distance at speeds from 30 to 70 miles per hour, in steps of 5 miles per hour. Read the distance.

    Formula

    $T=\dfrac{D}{S}$

    T: time (hours) D: distance (miles)
    S: speed (miles per hour)

11. A shop gives a cash discount on its goods. Print a table of the price, discount and price less discount for prices from £1 to £20 in steps of 50p. Read the discount rate.

    Formulae

    $D=\dfrac{P\times R}{100}$ $L=P-D$

    D: discount (£) P: price (£)
    R: discount rate (%) L: price less discount

□ 12. Find out the conversion rates for pounds sterling to some of these currencies: dollars, marks, French francs, Swiss francs, lire.

Print a conversion table for sterling to the other currencies, over the range £1 to £20.

Formulae

$D = R \times P$

D: dollars
R: dollar conversion rate (if £1 = \$1·75, then $R = 1·75$) P: pounds

$M = S \times P$

M: marks S: mark conversion rate P: pounds

The formulae for the other currencies are similar.

Section 2E
Using data repeatedly

It is often necessary to use the data more than once during the running of a program. The instruction RESTORE sends the computer back to the first data item. The example shows one way of using this instruction.

Example 2E

The monthly running costs of a factory are:

Materials	£3769
Wages	£4527
Administration	£1916
Transport	£417
Fuel	£215
Rent	£672
Other	£498

Calculate the total expenses, and the percentage which each item makes of the total. Print a table with headings:

ITEM   COST   PERCENTAGE OF TOTAL

Formula

$$P = \frac{C \times 100}{T}$$

P: percentage C: cost (£) T: total (£)

Method
The data must be read twice, once to calculate the total, and the second time to calculate the percentages. There must be two loops (using counters K and L, each from 1 to 7).

Before the first loop, the total is set to zero. In the first loop, the data is read and the total added up.

Between the loops, the instruction RESTORE starts the computer from the first data item again. The headings are printed at this stage.

In the second loop, the data is read again, each percentage calculated, and the required information printed.

Flow diagram

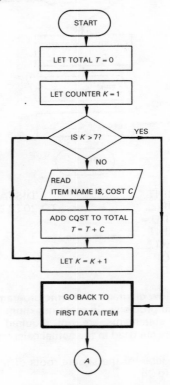

Note: A circle with a letter inside is used to connect the parts of the flow diagram.

Variables
K: first loop counter (1 to 7)
L: second loop counter (1 to 7) $I\$$: item name
C: cost (£) T: total cost (£) P: percentage

Results

ITEM	COST (£)	PERCENT OF TOTAL
MATERIALS	3769	31.377
WAGES	4527	37.6873
ADMIN	1916	15.9507
TRANSPORT	417	3.47153
ENERGY	213	1.77323
RENT	672	5.59441
OTHER	498	4.14585
TOTAL	12012	100

Points to notice

● The two loops must have different counters.

● The same variables (I$ and C) may be used in both loops for the items and costs.

● The item names must be read in the first loop even though they are not used.

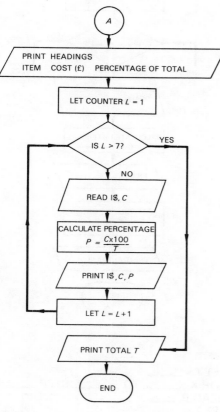

Program

```
5 LET T=0
10 FOR K=1 TO 7 STEP 1
15 READ I$,C
20 LET T=T+C
25 NEXT K
30 RESTORE
35 PRINT "ITEM","COST (£)","PERCENT OF TOTAL"
40 FOR L=1 TO 7 STEP 1
45 READ I$,C
50 LET P=C/T*100
55 PRINT I$,C,P
60 NEXT L
65 PRINT "TOTAL",T,"100"
70 STOP
75 DATA "MATERIALS",3769
80 DATA "WAGES    ",4527
85 DATA "ADMIN    ",1916
90 DATA "TRANSPORT", 417
95 DATA "ENERGY   ", 213
100 DATA "RENT     ", 672
105 DATA "OTHER    ", 498
110 END
*
```

Exercise 2E

Copy and complete the flow diagram and program for this problem.

1. The checking process at a factory making motor car pistons is as follows:

At intervals a piston is removed from the production line and its diameter measured. The reference number for each piston and its diameter are printed on data cards.

Write a program to read the information from six cards, calculate the average diameter, and then the difference between each diameter and the average. Print a table of reference numbers, diameters and differences.

Method

In the first loop, the data is read and the average calculated (see previous example).

In the second loop, the data is read again and the differences calculated. The references, diameters and differences are printed.

Flow diagram

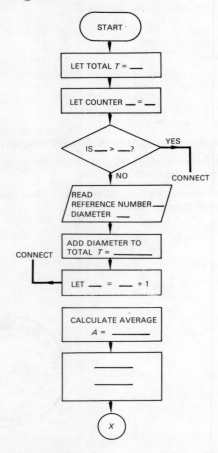

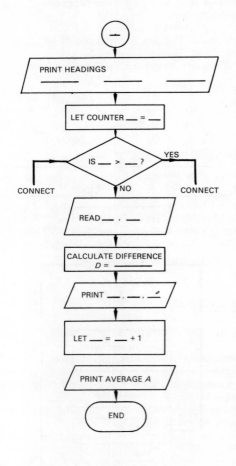

Variables

T: total of diameters   R: reference number
D: diameter (cm)   A: average diameter (cm)
E: difference between diameter and average
K: loop counter   L: loop counter

Program

```
  5 LET T=_____
 10 FOR K=_____ TO _____ STEP _____
 15 READ R, _____
 20 LET T=_____
 25 NEXT _____
 30 LET A=_____
 35 _____
 40 PRINT "_____", "DIAMETER  (CM)",
                          "_____"
 45 FOR L=_____ TO _____ STEP _____
 50 READ _____, _____
 55 LET E=_____
 60 PRINT _____, _____, _____
 65 NEXT "_____"
 70 PRINT "AVERAGE", _____
 75 _____
 80 DATA 3172, 8·61
 85 DATA _____, 8·60
 90 DATA _____, _____
 95 DATA _____, _____
100 DATA _____, _____
105 DATA _____, _____
110 END
```

Draw flow diagrams and write programs for some of these problems.

2. A circular diagram is to be made of a set of ten quantities. Read the quantities, calculate their total, and then the angle each will have on the diagram.

Formula

$$A = \frac{Q \times 360}{T}$$

A: angle (degrees) Q: quantity
T: total of the quantities

3. A grant of £75000 is to be shared amongst five schools in proportion to the number of pupils in each. Read the name of each school and its number of pupils. Calculate the total number of pupils. Then read the data a second time and calculate the share each school gets. Print a table headed:

SCHOOL PUPILS SHARE

Formula

$$S = \frac{N \times 75000}{T}$$

S: share (£) N: number of pupils T: total pupils

4. At a factory producing paint tins, a sample of twelve tins is selected every hour. The diameter and height of each tin is measured (in centimetres). Write a program to read this information (one line of data contains the reference number, diameter and height for a tin) and calculate the average diameter and average height. Then read the data again and calculate the difference between the diameter and height of each tin and the respective average. Print a table with headings

REF. NO. DIAMETER (CM) DIFFERENCE (CM)
         HEIGHT (CM) DIFFERENCE (CM)
Print the average diameter and average height underneath.

5. The monthly average sunshine hours in England and Wales in 1974 were:

	Hours of sunshine per day		Hours of sunshine per day
January	1·73	July	5·41
February	2·33	August	6·08
March	3·41	September	4·71
April	5·11	October	2·89
May	5·69	November	1·80
June	6·65	December	1·51

Read this information and calculate the average hours of sunshine per day for the year.

Then read the information again and calculate the percentage by which each month's figures differ from the average for the year.

Formula

$$P = \frac{(M-A) \times 100}{A}$$

P: percentage difference M: monthly average
A: average for the year

Print a table under the headings:

HOURS OF SUNSHINE PER DAY IN ENGLAND AND WALES, 1974
MONTH HOURS % DIFFERENCE
                    FROM AVERAGE
Print the average underneath.

Section 2F
Loops of variable length

A program loop may be of a variable length (and step size), as is shown in the following example.

Example 2F

A transport firm keeps its records as follows: Each truck journey is recorded on a data card with journey number, truck number, driver number and miles covered. At the end of a week, all the cards are read, the total mileage calculated, and the information printed in a suitable table.

Method

A separate data card is prepared with the number of journey cards. This card is read first, as the variable N.

A loop is used, with N as the limit, to read and print the information and add up the total.

Flow diagram

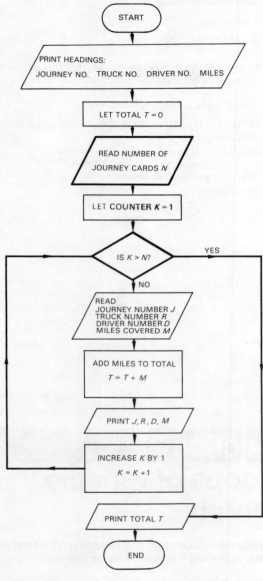

START

PRINT HEADINGS:

JOURNEY NO.   TRUCK NO.   DRIVER NO.   MILES

LET TOTAL $T = 0$

READ NUMBER OF
JOURNEY CARDS N

LET COUNTER $K = 1$

IS $K > N$? — YES

NO

READ
JOURNEY NUMBER J
TRUCK NUMBER R
DRIVER NUMBER D
MILES COVERED M

ADD MILES TO TOTAL
$T = T + M$

PRINT J, R, D, M

INCREASE K BY 1
$K = K + 1$

PRINT TOTAL T

END

Variables

T: total mileage N: number of journeys
K: counter (1 to N) J: journey number
R: truck number D: driver number
M: miles covered

Program

```
5 PRINT "JOURNEY NUMBER","TRUCK NUMBER","DRIVER NUMBER","MILEAGE"
10 LET T=0
15 READ N
20 FOR K=1 TO N STEP 1
25 READ J,R,D,M
30 LET T=T+M
35 PRINT J,R,D,M
40 NEXT K
45 PRINT
50 PRINT "TOTAL MILEAGE:",T
55 STOP
60 DATA 3
65 DATA 416,21,18,186
70 DATA 298,20,7,45
75 DATA 348,18,15,413
80 END
```

Results

JOURNEY NUMBER	TRUCK NUMBER	DRIVER NUMBER	MILEAGE
416	21	18	186
298	20	7	45
348	18	15	413

TOTAL MILEAGE: 644

Points to notice

● The first data card contains the number of journeys (here three). There must be this number of journey cards to follow.

Exercise 2F

Copy and complete the flow diagram and program for this problem:

1. Each week a machine parts factory receives a number of orders and prepares its production schedule from these orders. The data card for each order contains an order number, part number, cost and production time. Read the number of orders from a separate data card, then read the information for each order and print it. Calculate the total cost and total production time, and print these below the orders.

Method

● Variable N is first read as the number of orders, and used as the limit of the loop.

● The total cost T and total production time U are set to zero. The headings are printed.

● Inside the loop, the data is read and printed, and the totals added up.

● After the loop, the totals are printed.

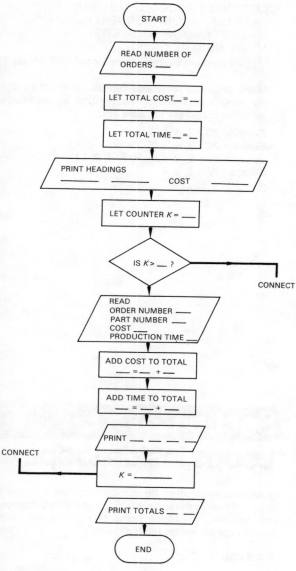

Variables

N: number of orders   T: total cost (£)
U: total time (hours)   K: counter
R: order number   P: part number
C: cost (£)   T: production time (hours)

```
 5 READ _____
10 LET ____ = ____
15 LET ____ = ____
20 PRINT  "_____",  "_____",  "COST",
                                    "_____"
25 FOR K = ____ TO ____ STEP ____
30 READ ____, ____, ____, ____
35 LET ____ = ____ + ____
40 LET ____ = ____ + ____
45 PRINT ____, ____, ____, ____
50 NEXT ____
55 PRINT "TOTALS",, ____, ____
60 STOP
65 DATA 4
70 DATA 613, 427, 67·93, 14
75 DATA ____, ____, ____, ____
80 DATA ____, ____, ____, ____
85 DATA ____, ____, ____, ____
90 END
```

Note: The extra comma in line 55 lines up the totals in their correct columns.

Draw flow diagrams and write programs for some of these problems. The first data item must be the length of the loop. This will determine the amount of data to follow.

2. A list is prepared of the names and dates of birth of the pupils in a form. A typical data card is

   55 DATA "JOAN EMMETT", "21/03/63"

   Write a program to read the number of pupils in the form, then read and print the name and date of birth of each.

3. Read the name, fuel consumption (miles per gallon) and the price per gallon of the fuel used, for a number of cars. For each car work out the number of gallons needed to travel 100 miles, and the cost.

   Formulae

   $$N = \frac{100}{F} \qquad\qquad C = N \times P$$

   N: number of gallons for 100 miles
   F: fuel consumption
   C: cost (£) of petrol for 100 miles
   P: petrol price (£) per gallon

   Print a table headed:

   PETROL USED AND COST FOR A 100 MILE
   JOURNEY BY DIFFERENT TYPES OF CAR
   TYPE MPG PETROL PRICE GALLONS USED
                                     COST

4. At the end of a term, the marks for the various pieces of work done by each pupil in a class are added up. Each total is out of a different amount, from some pupils having been absent. Read the number of pupils in the class, and then a data card for each

pupil, with name, total and what the total is out of. Calculate each pupil's percentage.

Formula

$$P = \frac{T \times 100}{M}$$

T: total mark
M: total possible mark (mark out of)
P: percentage

Print a table headed:

NAME   TOTAL   OUT OF   PERCENTAGE

Modification

Calculate and print the class average percentage.

□ 5. Write a program to calculate the sum of the squares of the numbers up to a certain number, which is read.

(If the number read is 4, then the sum is

$1^2 + 2^2 + 3^2 + 4^2 = 1 + 4 + 9 + 16 = 30$.)

6. A building is to be carpeted with carpet tiles, each of area 0·25 square metres. Write a program to read the number of rooms, then the length and breadth of each room (in metres) and calculate its area. Add up the total area, and calculate the number of tiles required for the building.

Formulae

$A = L \times B$
$N = \dfrac{T}{0 \cdot 25}$

A: area (m²) L: length (m) B: breadth
N: number of tiles T: total area

Print the length, breadth and area of each room, the total area and the number of tiles required.

7. When a customer at a certain garage buys motor car spare parts, data cards are punched to record the sale as follows:

(a) A customer header card showing:

(i) his customer account number, and
(ii) how many different types of spare parts were bought (e.g. tyre, an engine, a windscreen, etc.)

(b) A card for each different part purchased, showing (in this order)

(i) the part number
(ii) the price of a single part, and
(iii) the quantity of these parts bought

Write a BASIC program which reads these cards, and calculates the cost of each type of part purchased and the total bill.

The invoice to be printed is to have the headings as set out below. A flowchart may be drawn, though marks will not be awarded for it in this question.

CUSTOMER ACCOUNT NUMBER:
PART NO.   UNIT PRICE (£)
QUANTITY BOUGHT   COST (£)
TOTAL COST (£):

(East Anglian Examinations Board CSE Mode 3)

Many previous programs can be modified to alter the length of the loop by reading an additional variable. Especially suitable are:

Exercise 2B: 3, 4, 5, 7
Exercise 2C: 3, 4, 5, 6, 7
Exercise 2D: 2, 3, 4, 5, 6, 7, 8, 9, 11
Exercise 2E: 1, 2, 4

Section 2G
Loops inside loops

Processes must often be carried out over a range of values of two of the variables. Each variable becomes a loop counter, the loops being one inside the other. Such loops are called *nested loops*.

Example 2G1

At a car showroom, the salesmen keep records of their weekly total sales. Each month a data card is prepared for each salesman, with his name and sales figures for the four weeks. Write a program to read this information for five salesmen and print a table of it.

Method

A counter S from 1 to 5 controls the loop for the salesmen.

For each salesman, a counter W from 1 to 4 controls the loop to read and print the sales figures. This loop is inside the salesmen loop.

Suitable headings are:

SALESMAN   WEEK 1   WEEK 2   WEEK 3   WEEK 4

Flow diagram

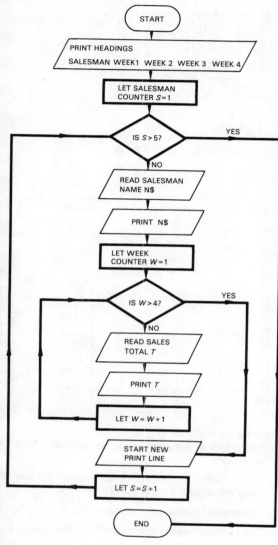

Variables

S: salesman counter (1 to 5)
N$: name of salesman
W: week counter (1 to 4)   T: weekly sales

Program

```
5  PRINT "SALESMAN","WEEK 1","WEEK 2","WEEK 3","WEEK 4"
10 FOR S=1 TO 5 STEP 1
15 READ N$
20 PRINT N$,
25 FOR W=1 TO 4 STEP 1
30 READ T
35 PRINT T,
40 NEXT W
45 PRINT
50 NEXT S
55 STOP
60 DATA "J.MACLEAN",4613,6331,5161,2977
65 DATA "K.CONWAY ",3161,5917,4813,3416
70 DATA "D.JARVIS ",5126,4617,6118,7161
75 DATA "E.SMITH  ",3814,7117,2090,4181
80 DATA "P.ROBERTS",4116,2080,3151,1270
85 END
*
```

Results

SALESMAN	WEEK 1	WEEK 2	WEEK 3	WEEK 4
J.MACLEAN	4613	6331	5161	2977
K.CONWAY	3161	5917	4813	3416
D.JARVIS	5126	4617	6118	7161
E.SMITH	3814	7117	2090	4181
P.ROBERTS	4116	2080	3151	1270

Points to notice

● The commas on the ends of PRINT statements 20 and 35 cause the output to stay on the same line, working across the columns.

● The word PRINT on its own in line 45 starts a new line.

Example 2G2

Credit terms are offered by a shop:

● a deposit of 15% of the cash price

● the rest paid in equal monthly instalments over 3, 6, 9 or 12 months.

Print a table of cash price, deposit and monthly instalments over the four repayment periods, for cash prices from £5 to £100 in steps of £5.

Formulae

$$D = \cdot 15 \times P$$
$$M = \frac{P - D}{N}$$

D: deposit (£)   P: cash price (£)
M: monthly instalment (£)
N: number of monthly instalments

Method

The price (variable P) is a loop counter from 5 to 100 in steps of 5. In this loop P is printed and the deposit calculated and printed.

The number of monthly instalments (variable N) is a loop counter from 3 to 12 in steps of 3, inside the prices loop. In this loop the monthly instalments (variable M) are calculated and printed.

Flow diagram

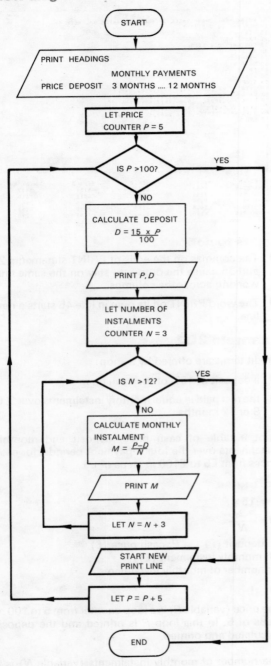

Variables
P: price (£) D: deposit (£)
N: number of instalments
M: monthly instalment (£)

Program

```
5 PRINT ,,"MONTHLY PAYMENTS"
10 PRINT "PRICE","DEPOSIT","3 MONTHS","6 MONTHS",
15 PRINT
20 FOR P=5 TO 100 STEP 5
25 LET D=15/100*P
30 PRINT P,D,
35 FOR N=3 TO 12 STEP 3
40 LET M=(P-D)/N
45 PRINT M,
50 NEXT N
55 PRINT
60 NEXT P
65 STOP
70 END
*
```

Results

PRICE	DEPOSIT	MONTHLY PAYMENTS 3 MONTHS	6 MONT
5	.75	1.41667	.7083
10	1.5	2.83333	1.416
15	2.25	4.25	2.125
20	3	5.66667	2.833
25	3.75	7.08333	3.541
30	4.5	8.5	4.25
35	5.25	9.91667	4.958
40	6	11.3333	5.666
45	6.75	12.75	6.375
50	7.5	14.1667	7.083
55	8.25	15.5833	7.791
60	9	17	8.5
65	9.75	18.4167	9.208
70	10.5	19.8333	9.916
75	11.25	21.25	10.62
80	12	22.6667	11.3
85	12.75	24.0833	12.00
90	13.5	25.5	12.75
95	14.25	26.9167	13.45
100	15	28.3333	14.16

Points to notice

- The NEXT M statement must be before the NEXT P statement.

- The commas at the end of statements 30 and 45 keep the output on the same line.

- Statement 55 starts a new print line.

- The two commas in statement 5 put the heading in the third column.

- No data is read in this program, and both loop counters occur in the calculations. Compare this with the previous example.

- In terms of the layout of the output, the inner loop works across the page and the outer loop down the page. This is a general pattern for nested loops.

```
"9 MONTHS","12 MONTHS"
```

MONTHS	12 MONTHS
.472222	.354167
.944444	.708333
.41667	1.0625
.88889	1.41667
2.36111	1.77083
2.83333	2.125
3.30556	2.47917
5.77778	2.83333
.25	3.1875
.72222	3.54167
5.19444	3.89583
5.66667	4.25
.13889	4.60417
.61111	4.95833
.08333	5.3125
.55556	5.66667
.02778	6.02083
.5	6.375
.97222	6.72917
.44444	7.08333

Exercise 2G

Copy and complete the flow diagram and program for this problem.

1. Print a table of the discount at 5%, 10%, 15% and 20% on amounts from £1 to £25 in steps of £1.

Formula

$$D = \frac{R \times A}{100}$$

D: discount (£) R: rate (%) A: amount (£)

Method

For each amount there are four discount rates. The amount must be the counter for the outer loop, the discount rate the counter for the inner loop.

The output layout is:

AMOUNT	DISCOUNT RATE			
	5%	10%	15%	20%
1				
2				
...				

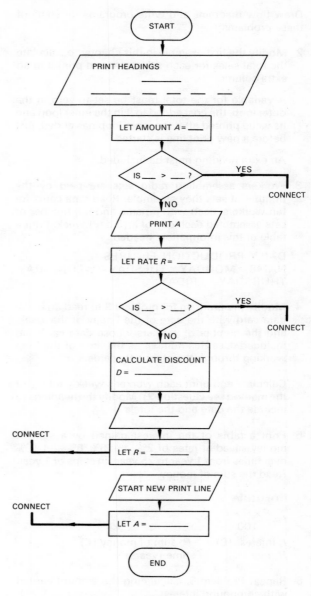

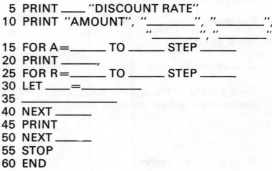

```
 5 PRINT ____ "DISCOUNT RATE"
10 PRINT "AMOUNT", "_____", "_____",
                   "_____", "_____"
15 FOR A=____ TO ____ STEP ____
20 PRINT ____,
25 FOR R=____ TO ____ STEP ____
30 LET ____=_____
35 _____
40 NEXT ____
45 PRINT
50 NEXT ____
55 STOP
60 END
```

33

Draw flow diagrams and write programs for some of these problems:

2. Modify the first example in this chapter to calculate the total sales for each salesman, and print it in an extra column.

A variable for the total must be set to zero in the outer loop, the cost added to it in the inner loop and its value printed after the inner loop has ended, just before a new print line is started.

An extra heading must be included.

3. Workers assembling radio sets are paid by the number of sets they assemble. Read data cards for ten workers, each with a name and the number of sets assembled each day of a (5 day) week. Print a table of this information, headed:

DAILY PRODUCTION FIGURES
NAME MONDAY TUESDAY WEDNESDAY
THURSDAY FRIDAY

☐ 4. Modify the program for problem 3 to read an initial data card with the date of the Friday of the week, and the number of workers whose data cards are included. Use this number as the limit of the loop working through the other data cards.

Calculate and print each worker's weekly total (for the method see Question 2). Modify the headings to include the date and the totals.

5. Print a table of the interest gained by a sum of money saved at rates of 2%, 4%, 6%, 8% and 10% over times from 1 year to 25 years in steps of 1 year. Read the sum of money.

Formula
$$I = \frac{P \times R \times T}{100}$$
I: interest (£) P: sum of money (£)
R: rate (%) T: time (years)

6. Repeat Problem 5, calculating the amount earned with compound interest.

Formula
$$A = P \times (1 + \frac{R}{100})^T$$
A: amount (£)

7. Print a table of the square, cube, fourth, fifth and sixth roots of whole numbers from 1 to 50.

Formula
$$R = N^{1/K}$$
R: root N: number
K: order of root. $K=2$ for square roots, 3 for cube roots, etc.

Several previous programs can be modified, using nested loops, to do the calculations over a range of values of two variables.

Exercise 2H

Draw flow diagrams and write programs for some of these problems. They combine the various methods introduced in this chapter.

1. Make a list of the name, channel, day and time of your five favourite TV programmes. Write a program to read this information from data cards and print a table of it. A typical data card is:

65 DATA "TOP OF THE POPS", "BBC 1", "THURSDAY", 7.20

Use variables:

N\$: name   C\$: channel   D\$: day
T: time K: counter (1 to 5)

2. Read the names and prices of six food items, and the prices of the same items some time ago (see for example the Daily Mirror Shopping Basket). For each item, calculate the percentage increase in price.

Formula
$$P = \frac{(C-R) \times 100}{R}$$
P: percentage increase C: present price
R: previous price

Print a table with headings:

ITEM PRESENT PRICE PREVIOUS PRICE
PERCENTAGE INCREASE

Modification

Calculate the total current price, total previous price and the percentage increase in these totals. Print this information below the table.

3. At a factory, the production cost of a TV set in terms of the number produced per week is
$$C = 20 + \frac{5000}{N} + \frac{N}{100}$$
C: cost (£) N: number produced per week

The sets are sold for £85 each. For production from 50 to 1000 sets per week, in steps of 50, calculate the cost of a set, the profit on one set, the total cost and the total profit. Print all this information in a table.

Formulae
$$P = 85 - C$$
$$S = C \times N$$
$$R = P \times N$$
P: profit (£) on one set S: total cost (£)
R: total profit (£)

4. The depth of an oil well after a number of days of drilling is

$$D = 5000\ (1 - 2\cdot72^{-7/50})$$

D: depth (metres) T: number of days drilling

Print a table of depths every 5 days up to 50 days.

5. For a positive whole number N, N factorial (written $N!$) is $1 \times 2 \times 3 \times \ldots \times N$ (e.g. $4! = 1 \times 2 \times 3 \times 4 = 24$). Write a program to calculate $N!$ for any input N.

6. When a house is bought on a mortgage, repayments are made (usually once a month) so that at the end of a certain period of time (usually from 5 to 30 years) the money borrowed and the interest charged has been paid back. The formula for the amount paid back per year is:

$$A = P \times K^N \times \left(\frac{1-K}{1-K^N}\right)$$

where $K = 1 + \dfrac{R}{100}$

   R: interest rate (%)
   P: amount borrowed (£)
   N: number of years of repayment
   A: amount paid back per year (£)

The total amount paid back is:

$$T = N \times A$$

T: total amount repaid (£)

Read in the amount borrowed, and the interest rate.

Calculate the amount paid back per year, and the total amount paid back, for periods of repayment from 5 to 30 years. Set out all the information in a table, with suitable headings.

7. Rewrite this program, correcting all the mistakes:

```
 5 PRINT 'CALCULATING THE TOTAL COST
10 FOR N=1 TO 5, STEP 1
15 READ N, P
20 LET C=NP
25 LET T=T+C
30 NEXT C
35 STOP.
40 DATA 4, 3·25, 5, 6·16, 9, 5·28, 7·11, 18, 7·8,
50 END
```

8. Write a list of the values of all the variables during the running of this program:

```
 5 LET T=0
10 LET N=1
15 FOR K=1 TO 3 STEP 1
20 LET N=N/2
25 LET T=T+N
30 PRINT N, T
35 NEXT K
40 STOP
45 END
```

Make a table with the following headings:

Line number	T	N	K	
5	0	—	—	
10	0	1	—	
15	0	1	1	etc.

Lines 15 to 35 will be repeated 3 times. Remember K increases its value at line 35.

Such a table is called a trace table, and the process a dry check. Do dry checks on other programs, and see if they agree with the actual printout.

9. In a race involving ten (10) runners, the times in seconds of the individual runners were recorded as they passed the winning post in finishing order.

Draw a flowchart and write a program in a high-level language

(a) to input the ten times in seconds into an array,
(b) to output
   (i) the average time
   (ii) those times which are greater than the average time.

Credit will be given for good output layout.

(Welsh Joint Education Committee)

10. (a) Explain *briefly* how you would document a program.

(b) The following flowchart calculates the area of a triangle using Heron's formula:

$$\text{area} = \sqrt{S(S-A)(S-B)(S-C)}$$
$$\text{where } S = (A+B+C)/2$$

(i) *Amend* the flowchart so that the processes can be performed a specified number of times.
(ii) Code the amended flowchart in a high-level language.

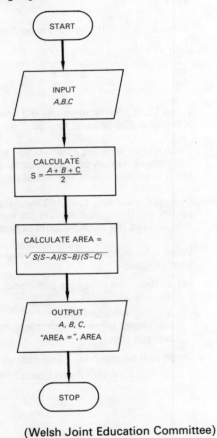

(Welsh Joint Education Committee)

11. (i) The flowchart shown does not include the headings in the print statements. Write a program in BASIC from the flowchart inserting suitable headings.
(ii) Explain the reason for the program and show precisely the output produced for $K=3$.

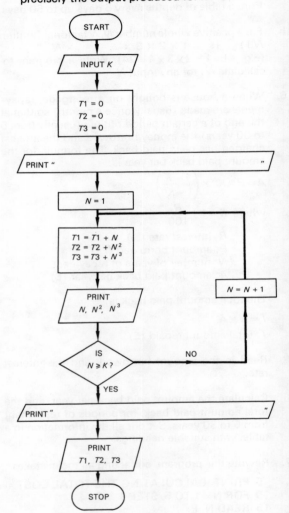

(University of Cambridge,
Local Examinations Syndicate)

3. More about variables, numbers and output

In this chapter, ideas introduced previously are studied in more detail. A method of printing graphs and histograms on a computer is also shown.

Section 3A
Variables and numbers

In addition to single letters, variables may be written as letters followed by single numbers: ·

e.g. A3 B5 Z9   are correct variables
      A10 AB 3A   are incorrect variables

Variables representing words, sometimes called *literal variables* may also include a number.

e.g. A3$ N4$ K9$ are correct variables
      B$4 AC$ 3A$ are incorrect variables

On some systems there may be a pound sign instead of a dollar sign.

e.g. K£ T£ A4£   are correct variables.

If a pound sign is permitted, A$ and A£ are the same variable.

Very large or very small numbers are conveniently written using powers of ten (standard form). In BASIC language, the letter E is used to show powers of ten.

Number	Standard form	BASIC
1 000 000	10^6	1E6
385 000 000	3.85×10^8	3.85E8
·000 1	10^{-4}	1E−4
·000 52	5.2×10^{-4}	5.2 E−4
−·000 067 71	-6.771×10^{-5}	−6.771 E−5

Numbers may be written in the E notation in data statements or in calculations in programs.

Example
Three propulsion systems are proposed for a spacecraft to visit the planet Pluto 3573 million miles away.

(3.573×10^9 miles.) The average speeds are:

type 1:   32000 mph (3.2×10^4)
type 2: 134000 mph (1.34×10^5)
type 3:   87500 mph (8.75×10^4)

Write a program to read the names of the types and their speeds. Calculate and print the time (hours) to reach the planet.

Formula
time = distance ÷ speed
i.e. time = 3.573×10^9 ÷ speed.

Method
A loop is not used. There are different variables for each type. All the data is read first, and then there are separate calculations and PRINT statements for each type.

Flow diagram

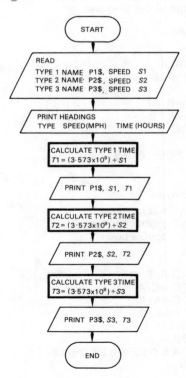

Variables

P1\$, P2\$, P3\$: three types
$S1$, $S2$, $S3$: three speeds
$T1$, $T2$, $T3$: three times

Program

```
 5 READ P1$,S1,P2$,S2,P3$,S3
10 PRINT "TYPE","SPEED(MPH)","TIME(HOURS)"
15 LET T1=3.573E9/S1
20 PRINT P1$,S1,T1
25 LET T2=3.573E9/S2
30 PRINT P2$,S2,T2
35 LET T3=3.573E9/S3
40 PRINT P3$,S3,T3
45 STOP
50 DATA "TYPE 1",3.2E4
55 DATA "TYPE 2",1.34E5
60 DATA "TYPE 3",8.75E4
65 END
*
```

Results

TYPE	SPEED(MPH)	TIME(HOURS)
TYPE 1	32000	111656
TYPE 2	134000	26664.2
TYPE 3	87500	40834.3

Points to notice

● This program could have been written a different way using a loop.

Exercise 3A

Copy these tables and fill in the values of the variables at each stage of the programs.

Example

	A	B	C	D	E
5 READ A, B	2.0×10^5	6.0×10^9			
10 LET C=A*B	2.0×10^5	6.0×10^9	12.0×10^{14} $= 1.2 \times 10^{15}$		
15 LET D=B/A	2.0×10^5	6.0×10^9	1.2×10^{15}	3.0×10^4	
20 LET E=A↑2	2.0×10^5	6.0×10^9	1.2×10^{15}	3.0×10^4	4.0×10^{10}
25 PRINT C, D, E					
30 STOP					
35 DATA 2.0E5, 6.0E9					
40 END					

Rules for powers:

Multiplying: add powers
Dividing: subtract powers
Squaring: double powers

	A	B	C	D	E	F
1. 5 READ A, B, C						
10 LET D=C/A						
15 LET E=A*C						
20 LET F=B/C						
25 PRINT D, E, F						
30 STOP						
35 DATA 4.0 E3, 8.0 E8, 2.0 E6						
40 END						

                          N1   N2   N3   K   L   M

2.   5 READ N1, N2, N3
     10 LET K=N1∗N2/2
     15 LET L=6∗N1/N3
     20 LET M=N2/N3
     25 PRINT K, L, M
     30 STOP
     35 DATA 2·0E7, 6·0E5, 3·0E4
     40 END

Draw flow diagrams and write programs for some of these problems.

3. The Viking spacecraft travelled the 204 million ($2·04 \times 10^8$) miles from Earth to Mars in 320 days. Read this information, change the days to hours (multiply by 24) and calculate its average speed. (Speed=distance÷time.)

4. Light travels at 186 000 ($1·86 \times 10^5$) miles per second. Calculate the time for light from the Sun to reach the Earth, 93 million ($9·3 \times 10^7$) miles away. (Time (seconds)=distance÷speed.)

5. A proton is a particle found in the centre of atoms. It has mass $1·67 \times 10^{-24}$ kg, radius $2·3 \times 10^{-13}$ metres. Calculate its volume and density.

volume=$\frac{4}{3} \times 3·14159 \times$ radius³ (m³)
density=mass÷volume (kg/m³)

Section 3B
Layout of output

When a computer is used to prepare and print such things as wage slips or accounts, the layout of the output is very important. A computer can also be programmed to print graphs, again requiring careful layout.

Each line of output has a maximum of 120 characters, spaced ten to the inch. The output from a BASIC program is normally laid out in columns. There are either eight columns each fifteen characters wide, or six columns each twenty characters wide. On a terminal there are usually five columns of fifteen characters.

Spacing is normally achieved in PRINT statements by commas and semicolons:

● A comma in a PRINT statement puts the next piece of output in the next column.

● A semicolon in a PRINT statement causes the output to be more closely spaced, with the next number or letter following a few spaces after the end of the previous one. The spacing is not usually the same for numbers and letters, and columns cannot be formed using semicolons.

● A comma at the end of a PRINT statement causes the output from the next PRINT statement to be printed on the same line, in the next column.

● A semicolon at the end of a PRINT statement puts the next output closely spaced on the same line.

Calculations can be carried out in PRINT statements. For example, the statements

35 LET N=2
40 PRINT 1/N

give the output 0·5.

The following program shows various uses of PRINT statements, on a computer giving eight columns of fifteen characters.

```
  5  PRINT "PROGRAM TO ILLUSTRATE DIFFERENT LAYOUTS"
 10  PRINT
 15  PRINT
 20  READ A,B,C,D,E,F,G,H
 25  PRINT "COLUMN 1","COLUMN 2","COLUMN 3","COLUMN 4",
 30  PRINT "COLUMN 5","CO UMN 6","COLUMN 7","COLUMN 8"
 35  PRINT A,B,C,D,E,F,G,H
 40  PRINT
 45  FOR N=0.5 TO 4.0 STEP 0.5
 50  PRINT N,
 55  NEXT N
 60  PRINT
 65  FOR N1=0.5 TO 4.0 STEP 0.5
 70  PRINT N1∗N1,
 75  NEXT N1
 80  PRINT
 85  PRINT
 90  PRINT "CLOSE SPACING OF OUTPUT"
 95  PRINT A;B;C;D;E;F;G;H
100  PRINT
105  FOR M=0.5 TO 4.0 STEP 0.5
110  PRINT M;
115  NEXT M
120  PRINT
125  FOR M1=0.5 TO 4.0 STEP 0.5
130  PRINT 1/M1;
135  NEXT M1
140  STOP
145  DATA 5,69,3,150,37.545,.53E8,66.1234,0.009
150  END
*
```

Results

```
PROGRAM TO ILLUSTRATE DIFFERENT LAYOUTS

COLUMN 1        COLUMN 2        COLUMN 3        COLUMN 4        COLUMN 5        COLUMN 6        COLUMN 7        COLUMN 8
5               69              3               150             37.545          5.3E7           66.1234         9E-3

.5              1               1.5             2               2.5             3               3.5             4

.25             1               2.25            4               6.25            9               12.25           16


CLOSE SPACING OF OUTPUT
5 69 3 150  37.545  5.3E7  66.1234  9E-3

.5  1  1.5  2  2.5  3  3.5  4
2  1  .666667  .5  .4  .333333  .285714  .25
```

Points to notice

● The closely spaced numbers do not form columns. Each line is spaced according to the width of the numbers.

Exercise 3B

Write the PRINT statements which have produced this output, using variables $A=1$, $B=2$, $C=3$, $D=4$, $E=5$, $F=6$.

```
1               2               3               4               5               6
1     2               3     4         5     6
1     2     3     4     5     6
1               .5              .333333         .25             .2              .166667
```

Section 3C
Tabulating output

It is frequently inconvenient to use the standard columns, either because more than eight columns are required, or because columns wider than fifteen characters are wanted. The word TAB (for tabulate) in a PRINT statement causes output to be printed after a certain number of spaces. For Example:

● 15 PRINT TAB (20); "DATE"

puts the word DATE after 20 spaces.

● 35 LET N=30
   40 PRINT TAB (N); A

puts the value of A 30 spaces from the left.

● 20 FOR N=1 TO 10 STEP 1
   25 PRINT TAB (10*N); N;
   30 NEXT N

prints the numbers 1, 2, 3 . . . 10 across the page, starting 10, 20, 30 . . . 100 spaces from the left.

There must always be a semicolon after the word TAB.

Example 3C1

Read the names and annual salaries of six employees. Calculate the monthly salary (annual salary ÷12) of each. Print a table with headings:

NAME OF EMPLOYEE ANNUAL SALARY (£)
                       MONTHLY SALARY (£)

Method

The headings are too wide for ordinary columns. If each column is allowed 25 spaces, then the second column starts after 25 spaces and the third after 50 spaces. TAB instructions are used in printing the headings and the results.

Flow diagram

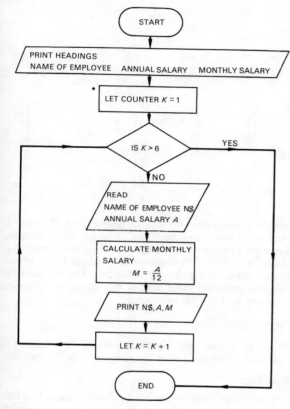

Variables

K: counter   N$: name of employee
A: annual salary (£)   M: monthly salary (£)

Program

```
5 PRINT "NAME OF EMPLOYEE";TAB(25);"ANNUAL SALARY (£)";
10 PRINT TAB(50);"MONTHLY SALARY (£)"
15 FOR K=1 TO 6 STEP 1
20 READ N$,A
25 LET M=A/12
30 PRINT N$;TAB(25);A;TAB(50);M
35 NEXT K
40 STOP
45 DATA "K.ROBINSON ",3165,"S.WINTERS  ",4529
50 DATA "M.RICHMOND ",2969,"P.EDGAR    ",3352
55 DATA "S.WATERFORD ",4162,"N.RAY      ",2768
60 END
```

Results

NAME OF EMPLOYEE	ANNUAL SALARY (£)	MONTHLY SALARY (£)
K.ROBINSON	3165	263.75
S.WINTERS	4529	377.417
M.RICHMOND	2969	247.417
P.EDGAR	3352	279.333
S.WATERFORD	4162	346.833
N.RAY	2768	230.667

Points to notice

● The READ and DATA statements contain commas only. Semicolons occur in PRINT statements only.

● One data card contains the information for two employees.

Example 3C2

Print a multiplication table for numbers from 1 to 10.

Method

Nested loops must be used, the outer one working down the table (counter A), the inner one working across (counter B). Each number C in the table will be

$$C = A \times B$$

The ten columns are best spaced every ten spaces across the page. Since the counter B works across the pages, TAB $(10 * B)$ will give the required columns.

Flow diagram

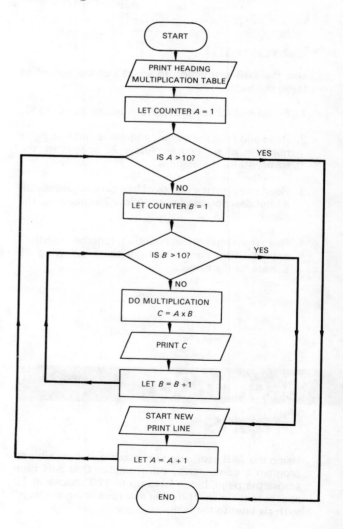

Program

```
 5 PRINT "MULTIPLICATION TABLE"
10 PRINT
15 FOR A=1 TO 10 STEP 1
20 FOR B=1 TO 10 STEP 1
25 LET C=A*B
30 PRINT TAB(10*B);C;
35 NEXT B
40 PRINT
45 NEXT A
50 STOP
55 END
*
```

Results

```
MULTIPLICATION TABLE
    1         2         3         4         5         6         7         8         9         10
    2         4         6         8         10        12        14        16        18        20
    3         6         9         12        15        18        21        24        27        30
    4         8         12        16        20        24        28        32        36        40
    5         10        15        20        25        30        35        40        45        50
    6         12        18        24        30        36        42        48        54        60
    7         14        21        28        35        42        49        56        63        70
    8         16        24        32        40        48        56        64        72        80
    9         18        27        36        45        54        63        72        81        90
    10        20        30        40        50        60        70        80        90        100
```

Exercise 3C

Use the TAB instruction to space out the output of these programs.

1. Print a multiplication table for numbers from 1 to 12.

2. Read and print the names, addresses and telephone numbers of six people. Allow 25 spaces for the name, 40 for the address.

3. Read and print the names of four cars, together with a brief description of each. Allow 20 spaces for the name.

4. Read the names of five countries, together with their capital cities. Print a table of these, allowing 25 spaces for the name.

Section 3D
Graphs

Using the TAB instruction for spacing, it is possible to program a computer to print graphs. One axis runs across the page. It can have up to 120 spaces, at 10 spaces to the inch. The other axis runs down the page, with six lines to the inch.

Graphs always contain two variables. One of these is usually a loop counter. The axis for this variable generally runs down the page. Spacing is achieved by using extra PRINT statements to produce blank lines. The other variable is usually calculated. The axis for this variable generally runs across the page. Spacing is achieved by the TAB instruction.

Example 3D1

Print a graph to convert metres to feet (1 metre=3·2808 feet) over the range of 1 to 10 metres.

Method

A loop is used with the metres as counter, from 1 to 10. The metres axis runs down the page, ten spaces in from the left. The spacing is one metre every two lines.

The feet are calculated from the equation

$F = 3 \cdot 2808 \times M$

F: feet M: metres

The feet run across the page. Since the largest number of feet is about 33, a convenient spacing is one foot every three spaces. Allowing ten spaces for the metres axis, the spacing instruction is TAB $(10+3*F)$.

The numbers for the feet axis are first printed across the page. The numbers for the metres axis are printed at the beginning of each line.

Flow diagram

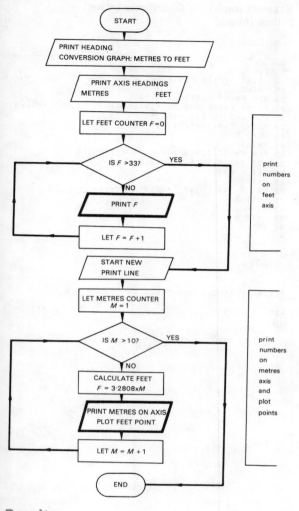

START

PRINT HEADING
CONVERSION GRAPH: METRES TO FEET

PRINT AXIS HEADINGS
METRES   FEET

LET FEET COUNTER F = 0

IS F > 33? — YES

NO

PRINT F

LET F = F + 1

START NEW
PRINT LINE

LET METRES COUNTER
M = 1

IS M > 10? — YES

NO

CALCULATE FEET
F = 3·2808×M

PRINT METRES ON AXIS,
PLOT FEET POINT

LET M = M + 1

END

print numbers on feet axis

print numbers on metres axis and plot points

Variables

F: feet   *M*: metres

Program

```
5 PRINT "CONVERSION GRAPH : METRES TO FEET "
10 PRINT
15 REM PRINT FEET AXIS
20 PRINT "METRES";TAB(50);"FEET"
25 FOR F=0 TO 33 STEP 3
30 PRINT TAB(10+3*F);F;
35 NEXT F
40 PRINT
45 REM PRINT METRES AXIS AND PLOT POINTS
50 FOR M=1 TO 10 STEP 1
55 LET F=3.2808*M
60 PRINT
65 PRINT TAB(10);M;TAB(10+3*F);"*"
70 NEXT M
75 STOP
80 END
*
```

Points to notice

● The variable *F* is used twice—first as a loop counter, then in a calculation.

● Line 60 prints a blank line to give the metres axis the correct spacing of two lines to a metre.

● Numbers on the feet axis start at 0 and not 1. Every third number is printed.

Example 3D2

Read the average speed of a train (not more than 80 mph) and print a graph of the distances it will travel over times up to six hours in steps of half an hour.

Method

The speed is read first. The time is a loop counter. Its axis runs down the page, with a spacing of four lines to one hour, or two lines to half an hour. It is printed ten spaces in from the side.

Results

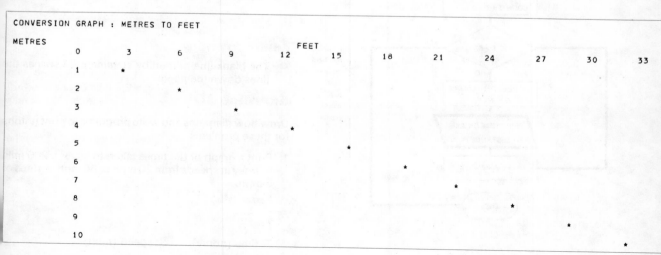

```
CONVERSION GRAPH : METRES TO FEET

METRES
          0        3        6        9       12      FEET 15      18       21       24       27       30       33
          1        *
          2                 *
          3                          *
          4                                   *
          5                                            *
          6                                                     *
          7                                                              *
          8                                                                       *
          9                                                                                *
         10                                                                                         *
```

Distances are calculated from

$$D = S \times T$$

S: speed (mph) T: time (hours)
D: distance (miles)

The maximum possible distance is 480 miles (80 mph for 6 hours), giving a convenient spacing of one space for five miles. This is achieved by TAB ($10 \times D/5$). The miles axis is first printed across the page in steps of 50 miles up to 500 miles.

Flow diagram

Variables

S: speed (mph) D: distance (miles)
T: time (hours)

Program

```
5 READ S
10 PRINT "TRAIN DISTANCES AND TIMES AT ";S;" M.P
15 PRINT
20 REM PRINT DISTANCE AXIS
25 PRINT "TIME (HOURS)";TAB(40);"DISTANCE (MILES
30 FOR D=0 TO 500 STEP 50
35 PRINT TAB(10+D/5);D;
40 NEXT D
45 PRINT
50 REM PRINT TIMES AND PLOT DISTANCES
55 FOR T=0.5 TO 6 STEP 0.5
60 LET D=S*T
65 PRINT
70 PRINT TAB(10);T;TAB(10+D/5);"*"
75 NEXT T
80 STOP
85 DATA 72
90 END
*
```

Results

```
TRAIN DISTANCES AND TIMES AT   72  M.P.H.

TIME (HOURS)                              DISTANCE
        0         50       100       150
       .5         *
        1              *
      1.5                  *
        2                       *
      2.5                           *
        3
      3.5
        4
      4.5
        5
      5.5
        6
```

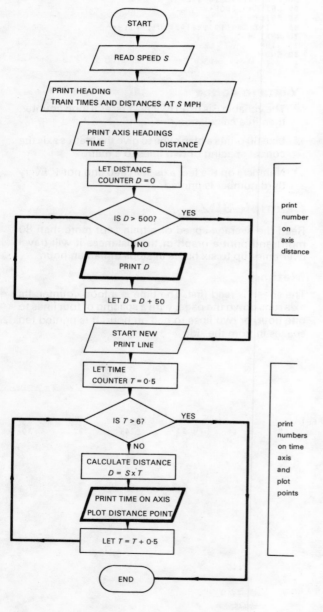

Points to notice

● The blank line printed by statement 65 spaces the lines down the page.

Exercise 3D

Draw flow diagrams and write programs to print graphs for these problems.

1. Print a graph of the times taken to cover a 200 mile journey at speeds from 20 mph to 60 mph in steps of 5 mph.

Formula

$$T = \frac{200}{S}$$

T: time (hours) S: speed (mph)

Modify this program to print conversion graphs to other currencies.

3. Refer to Exercise 2D for more conversion graphs.

4. The height of the cable of a suspension bridge at a distance D metres from one end of the main span is:

$$H = \frac{D \times (D - 100)}{50} + 55$$

The span is 100 m long and 55 m high at each end.

Print a graph of the curve of the cable, with distance running down the page (plot one point for every 5 metres) and height across the page (one space to one metre).

5. Plot the graph of $y = 20 - 2x$ for x from 1 to 10. The x axis runs down the page in steps of one unit every two lines. The y axis runs across the page, five spaces to one unit, ranging from 0 to 20.

| 50 | 300 | 350 | 400 | 450 | 500 |

Suggested layout:

● Time across the page, 10 spaces to 1 hour, use TAB $(10 + 10 * T)$, since the longest time is 10 hours.

● Speed down the page, 2 lines to 5 mph.

2. Read the current conversion rate from pounds to French francs, and print a conversion graph over the range £1 to £20 in steps of £1.

Formula

$F = R \times P$

F: francs P: pounds R: conversion rate
(if £1 = 8·92 francs, then $R = 8·92$)

(The conversion rate will probably not be more than £1 = 10 francs.)

Section 3E
Histograms

Histograms show information by lines or columns of different lengths. On a computer it is most convenient to have these columns running across a page. Nested loops are used in histogram programs, the outer loop to read the information and print it down the page, the inner loop to work across each line, printing the column to its required length.

A suitable scale must be chosen to fit the 120 spaces across the page. TAB instructions are not usually necessary.

Example 3E

Read the attendance figures for a form for the ten school sessions in a week. Print a histogram of them. The maximum attendance in the form is 30.

Method

A loop (counter S from 1 to 10) reads the session (Monday a.m., Monday p.m., etc.) and attendance (variable N). The session is printed, and then an inner loop (counter K from 1 to N) prints a symbol ($+$) for each pupil present.

A suitable spacing is two spaces per pupil, so a blank space is left after each $+$ sign.

45

Flow diagram

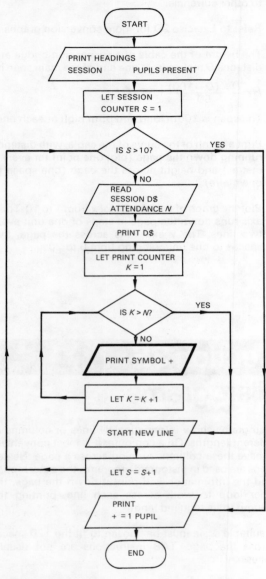

Variables

S: session counter (1 to 10)   D$: session name
K: print counter (1 to N) N: attendance

Program

```
5 PRINT "SESSION","PUPILS PRESENT"
10 PRINT
15 FOR S=1 TO 10 STEP 1
20 READ D$,N
25 PRINT D$,
30 FOR K=1 TO N STEP1
35 PRINT "+ ";
40 NEXT K
45 PRINT
50 NEXT S
55 PRINT
60 PRINT "+ = 1 PUPIL "
65 STOP
70 DATA "MON  A.M.",21,"MON  P.M.",20
75 DATA "TUES A.M.",24,"TUES P.M.",26
80 DATA "WED  A.M.",23,"WED  P.M.",23
85 DATA "THUR A.M.",21,"THUR P.M.",19
90 DATA "FRI  A.M.",22,"FRI  P.M.",21
95 END
```

Results

```
SESSION      PUPILS PRESENT

MON  A.M.    + + + + + + + + + + + + + + + + + + + + +
MON  P.M.    + + + + + + + + + + + + + + + + + + + +
TUES A.M.    + + + + + + + + + + + + + + + + + + + + + + + +
TUES P.M.    + + + + + + + + + + + + + + + + + + + + + + + + + +
WED  A.M.    + + + + + + + + + + + + + + + + + + + + + + +
WED  P.M.    + + + + + + + + + + + + + + + + + + + + + + +
THUR A.M.    + + + + + + + + + + + + + + + + + + + + +
THUR P.M.    + + + + + + + + + + + + + + + + + + +
FRI  A.M.    + + + + + + + + + + + + + + + + + + + + + +
FRI  P.M.    + + + + + + + + + + + + + + + + + + + + +

+ = 1 PUPIL
```

Points to notice

● The blank space after the + sign in statement 35 makes the spacing two spaces per pupil across the page.

Exercise 3E

Copy and complete the flow diagram and program for this problem:

1. The amount of oil refined in Britain each year from 1963 to 1973 was:

   1963: 50 million tons
   1964: 54 million tons
   1965: 66 million tons
   1966: 69 million tons
   1967: 72 million tons
   1968: 79 million tons
   1969: 90 million tons
   1970: 102 million tons
   1971: 104 million tons
   1972: 105 million tons
   1973: 112 million tons
   Draw a histogram of these figures.

Method

A counter Y from 1963 to 1973 reads the data (the amounts refined only).

A suitable scale is one symbol for 10 million tons spaced every four spaces across the page. The amount refined must be divided by ten to get the limit for the inner loop.

46

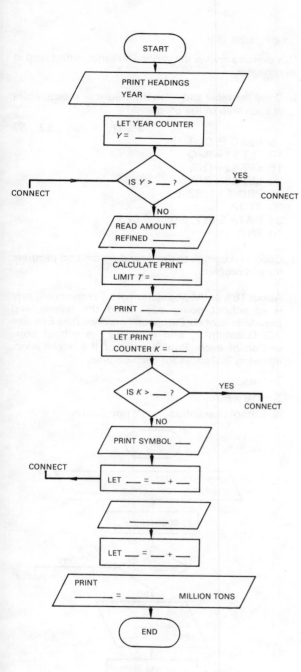

```
 5  PRINT   "YEAR",   "_____"
10  PRINT
15  FOR Y=_____ TO ___ STEP _____
20  READ _____
25  LET T=_____
30  PRINT _____,
35  FOR K=_____ TO _____ STEP _____
40  PRINT "_____" ___
45  NEXT _____
50  _____
55  NEXT _____
60  PRINT
65  PRINT "_____=_____ MILLION TONS"
70  STOP
75  DATA 50, ____, ____, ____, ____
80  _____
85  END
```

Draw flow diagrams and write programs for some of
these problems.

2. The price index numbers for Britain for the period
   1963 to 1973 were:

1963: 72·9		1969: 93·2
1964: 75·3		1970: 100·0
1965: 78·7		1971: 108·1
1966: 81·9		1972: 115·4
1967: 84·2		1973: 127·1
1968: 89·9		

   The figures mean that an article costing 100 pence
   in 1970 would, on average, have cost 72·9p in 1963
   and 127·1p in 1973.

   Read these figures, divide them by a suitable scale
   factor (say 2, then *=2 units) and print a histogram
   of them.

   Reference: *Britain 1975, an Official Handbook*
   (HMSO).

3. Using the information from the previous question,
   the inflation rate can be found by subtracting each
   price index from the following one:

   e.g.   1963: inflation=75·3−72·9=2·4%

   Work out these rates (or write part of your program
   to work them out) and print a histogram of them.
   Use a suitable scale (perhaps *=1%).

4. The following figures give indications of the relative access of people from different parts of the world to communications media. Write a program to draw histograms of some or all of them.

Daily newspapers (copies per 100 people)	Radios (sets per 100 people)	TV (sets per 100 people)	Telephones (sets per 100 people)	
10·5	18·5	6·3	6·8	World
4·2	3·7	1·2	1·4	Asia
25·8	28·0	15·9	12·0	Europe
1·1	4·4	0·2	0·9	Africa
6·5	15·1	4·0	2·7	S. America
23·8	102·3	28·5	52·7	N. America
29·5	34·2	9·6	14·1	USSR
29·6	21·0	17·1	26·5	Oceania

Reference: John McHale, *World Facts and Trends* (Collier)

5. In 1970, the number of computers in different countries was estimated as:

World	106 000
USA	62 500
West Germany	6 100
UK	5 900
Japan	5 900
France	4 500
USSR	5 500
Canada	3 000
Italy	2 700
Scandinavia	1 500
Netherlands	1 100

Reference: John McHale, *World Facts and Trends* (Collier)

Read these figures and print a histogram of them. Use the scale *=1000 computers.

6. If the inflation rate is a certain percentage, the price of an article over a number of years will follow the formula:

$$P = N\left(1 + \frac{R}{100}\right)^T$$

P: price (£) after T years N: price now (£)
R: inflation rate (%) T: time (years)

Read values of N and R, and print a histogram of the price of the article for each of the next twelve years.

Exercise 3F

This exercise revises the various methods introduced in this chapter.

1. Copy the table and fill in the values of the variables at each step of the program.

```
 5 READ P, Q, R
10 LET S1=P*Q
15 LET S2=Q/R
20 LET S3=R/P
25 PRINT S1, S2, S3
30 STOP
35 DATA 5·0E7, 6·0E5, 3·0E3
40 END
```

P	Q	R	S1	S2	S3

2. Copy and complete the flow diagram and program for this problem.

About 18% of the population of a European country is of school going age. Read the names and populations of six European countries (see Exercise 2C, Question 9) and calculate the school population of each. Print a table of the information, allowing 20 spaces for each column.

Formula

$S = \cdot 18 \times P$

S: school population P: population

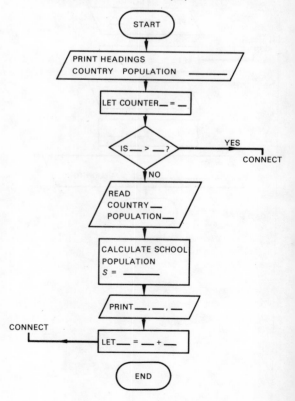

Variables

K: counter   N$: name of country
P: population (millions)
S: school population (millions)

```
 5 PRINT  "COUNTRY";  TAB  (____);
          "POPULATION";_____;"_____;"
10 FOR K=_____ TO _____ STEP _____
15 READ _____, _____
20 LET S=_____
25 PRINT _____, TAB (____); _____;
                TAB (____); _____
30 NEXT _____
35 STOP
40 DATA "_____",_____
45 DATA _____
50 _____
55 _____
60 _____
65 _____
70 END
```

Draw flow diagrams and write programs for some of these problems.

3. The six largest towns in Britain in 1971 were:

	Population
London	7 441 000
Birmingham	1 014 000
Glasgow	894 000
Liverpool	605 000
Manchester	546 000
Sheffield	518 000

Read this information, using the E notation for the populations, and print a list of it. Allow 20 spaces for the names of the towns.

For example: $605\,000 = 6 \cdot 05 \times 10^5 = 6 \cdot 05E5$

4. A coal truck can carry 16 tons of coal. Print a graph of the number of tons carried by coal trains of lengths 1 to 25 trucks.

Formula

$A = 16 \times B$

B: number of trucks   A: number of tons

Use a loop counter for the trucks (1 to 25 in steps of 1) with its axis down the page (1 line for each number of trucks), ten spaces from the left.

The maximum number of tons is 400, so one space to 4 tons will be a suitable scale. Print the tons axis across the page from 0 to 400 tons in steps of 40 tons.

5. The rainfall (in millimetres) for each month of 1974 in Wales was:

January	229	July	130
February	157	August	98
March	71	September	227
April	18	October	121
May	68	November	171
June	81	December	141

Read this information and print a histogram of it.

A suitable scale will be one symbol for 10 millimetres, every four spaces across the page.

6. Print a conversion table from feet and inches to metres, set out as shown:

FEET	INCHES	0	1	2	3	...	...	11
0		0	·0254					
1		·3048	...					
2		...	...	etc.				

Use nested loops: the inner one, counter I for inches from 0 to 11, the outer one, counter F for feet from 0 to 20.

Since 1 inch = ·0254 metres, multiply the feet by 12, add the inches and multiply by ·0254 .

$M = (12 \times F + I) \times \cdot 0254$

M: metres   F: feet   I: inches

There will be 13 columns. A spacing of nine spaces per column will be suitable.

4. Conditions

In many cases parts of a program must only be done under certain conditions. The statements which transfer control to various parts of a program under different conditions are now introduced.

Section 4A
IF and GO TO statements

The word IF is used to transfer control under a condition. For example:

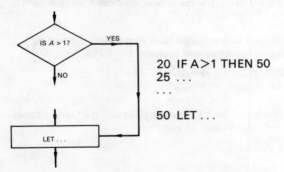

```
20 IF A>1 THEN 50
25 ...
...
50 LET ...
```

If *A* is greater than 1, control passes to statement 50, but if *A* is not greater than 1, control passes to statement 25.

An IF statement corresponds to a decision box in a flow diagram. In the flow diagram, the condition is expressed as a question, with different arrows for the answers YES and NO.

The words GO TO transfer control to another statement. For example:

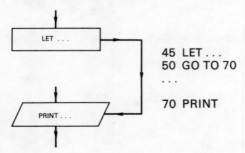

```
45 LET ...
50 GO TO 70
...
70 PRINT
```

Control passes from statement 50 to statement 70.

There is no flow diagram box corresponding to a GO TO statement. It is shown by the layout of the arrows.

Example 4A1

A salesman is entitled to a bonus of £10 unless his commission for a week's sales is less than £35. Input a salesman's name and commission, and add the bonus if necessary. Print the salesman's name and commission.

Method

The condition is:

is the commission less than £35?

If so, no bonus is added.

Flow diagram

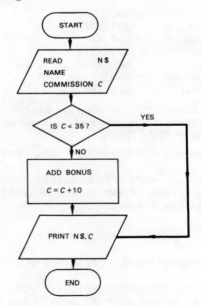

Variables

N$: name   C: commission

50

Program

```
*BASIC EXAMPLE 4A1

5   READ N$,C
10  IF C<35 THEN 20
15  LET C=C+10
20  PRINT "NAME", N$
25  PRINT "COMMISSION","£";C
30  STOP
35  DATA "C.ATKINSON",46.74
40  END
*
```

Results

NAME	C.ATKINSON
COMMISSION	£56.74

Points to notice

● Notice how the IF statement corresponds to the layout of the arrows in the flow diagram.

Example 4A2

A furniture removal firm has two sizes of vans: small vans for up to 30 items, large vans for more than 30 items. Read a job number and a number of items. Print this information, together with the message LARGE VAN or SMALL VAN as required.

Method

The most convenient condition is:

is the number of items more than 30?

in which case a large van is required.

Flow diagram

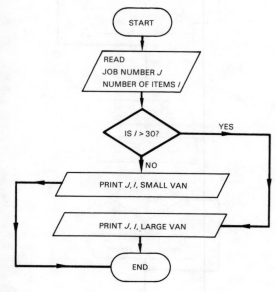

Variables

J: job number I: number of items

Program

```
5   READ J,I
10  IF I>30 THEN 25
15  PRINT "JOB:";J,"ITEMS:";I,"SMALL VAN"
20  GO TO 30
25  PRINT "JOB:";J,"ITEMS:";I,"LARGE VAN"
30  STOP
35  DATA 4617,46
40  END
*
```

Results

JOB: 4617	ITEMS: 46	LARGE VAN

Points to notice

● The GO TO statement prevents statement 25 being done when it is not wanted.

Relations used in IF ... THEN statements

A condition statement always contains a comparison between two quantities. If the comparison is true, control passes to the statement indicated after the word THEN. If the comparison is not true, control passes to the next statement.

The following relations may be used to express the comparisons:

Symbol	Meaning
$>$	greater than
$<$	less than
$> =$	greater than or equal to
$< =$	less than or equal to
$=$	equal to
$< >$ or $> <$	not equal to

Exercise 4A

Say whether or not control will pass to statement 50.

Example

IF A$>$2*B THEN 50
$A=11$ $B=50$

Comparison

$11>$ 2×5
$11>$ 10 ... true

Control will pass to statement 50:
Questions

1. IF 3*X<17 THEN 50	X=6
2. IF 10−Y><X+5 THEN 50	Y=4 X=0
3. IF X*X>100 THEN 50	X=9·9
4. IF 3*(A+B)/5=21 THEN 50	A=29 B=6
5. IF A+B>0 THEN 50	A=6 B=−9

Write program segments for these flow diagrams:

Example

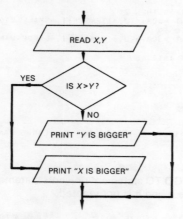

```
30  READ X, Y
35  IF X Y THEN 50
40  PRINT "Y IS BIGGER"
45  GO TO 55
50  PRINT "X IS BIGGER"
55  . . .
```

6.

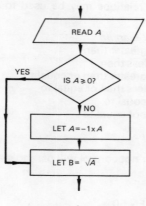

7.

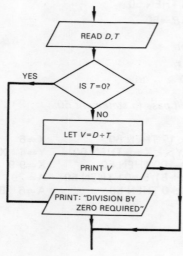

8.

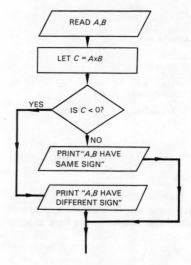

9.

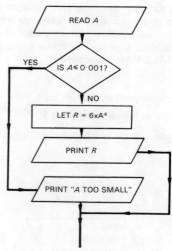

10.

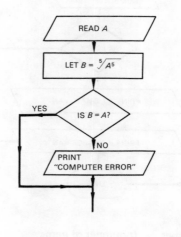

52

Draw flow diagrams and write programs for some of these problems:

11. A salesman is entitled to a £15 bonus unless his weekly sales are less than £200. Read the salesman's name, sales and weekly wage. Add the bonus to the wage if necessary. Print the name and weekly wage.

12. The heating system of a factory is switched on if the average temperature at three points is less than 13°C. Read three temperatures, find their average and print the average with the message HEATING ON or HEATING OFF as required.

13. A triangle is right angled if the relation $a^2 = b^2 + c^2$ holds for it, where a is the length of the longest side, b and c are the lengths of the other sides. Read the three lengths, and print them, with the words RIGHT ANGLED if required.

Section 4B
Conditions in loops

Conditions are usually used in conjunction with loops.

Example 4B1

At a timber yard, wood is dried until its moisture content is less than 15%. If so, it is ready to be cut. A data card is prepared for each of six samples, showing its stack number and moisture content. Read and print this information, with the message READY FOR CUTTING where required.

Method

Headings are printed:

STACK NO.   MOISTURE CONTENT (%)

A loop (counter N from 1 to 6) is used to work through the data. The condition

is the percentage less than 15%?

sorts the stacks which are ready to be cut. The data is printed, with the message if required.

Flow diagram

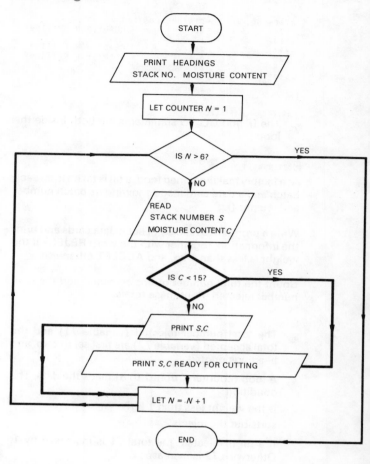

Variables

N: counter (1 to 6) S: stack number
C: moisture content

Program

```
5 PRINT "STACK NO.","MOISTURE CONTENT"
10 FOR N=1 TO 6 STEP 1
15 READ S,C
20 IF C<15 THEN 35
25 PRINT S,C
30 GO TO 40
35 PRINT S,C,"READY FOR CUTTING"
40 NEXT N
45 STOP
50 DATA 475,13
55 DATA 613,17
60 DATA  74,11
65 DATA 129, 8
70 DATA 518,23
75 DATA 117,15
80 END
*
```

Results

```
STACK NO.        MOISTURE CONTENT
   475               13            READY FOR CUTTING
   613               17
    74               11            READY FOR CUTTING
   129                8            READY FOR CUTTING
   518               23
   117               15
```

Points to notice
● The IF and GO TO statements are both inside the loop.

Example 4B2
At a factory making tinned food, a tin is taken from each batch and a data card made showing its batch number and weight (kg).

Write a program to read eight such data cards and print the information, together with the word REJECT if the weight is less than 1 kg, and ACCEPT otherwise.

Count the total number of tins accepted and the total number rejected. Print these totals.

Method
● The total number rejected (variable $T1$) and the total accepted (variable $T2$) are first set to zero, and headings printed.

● A loop (counter K from 1 to 8) reads the data. The condition:

 is the weight less than 1 kg?

 sorts out the rejects.

 If a tin is rejected, the total $T1$ is increased by 1. Otherwise $T2$ is increased by 1.

● After the loop, the two totals are printed.

Flow diagram

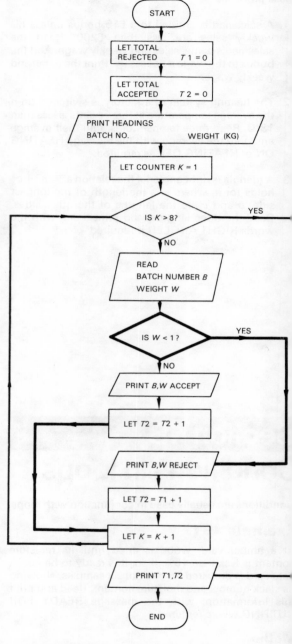

Variables
$T1$: total number of tins rejected
$T2$: total number of tins accepted
K: loop counter (1 to 8) B: batch number
W: weight (kg)

Program

```
5 LET T1=0
10 LET T2=0
15 PRINT "BATCH NO.","WEIGHT (KG)"
20 FOR K=1 TO 8 STEP 1
25 READ B,W
30 IF W<1 THEN 50
35 PRINT B,W,"ACCEPT"
40 LET T2=T2+1
45 GO TO 60
50 PRINT B,W,"REJECT"
55 LET T1=T1+1
60 NEXT K
65 PRINT "TOTAL REJECTED:";T1
70 PRINT "TOTAL ACCEPTED:";T2
75 STOP
80 DATA   4671,0.987
85 DATA   3918,1.012
90 DATA   2775,1.039
95 DATA   5161,0.991
100 DATA 0719,1.102
105 DATA 3127,1.009
110 DATA 4152,1.006
115 DATA 5163,0.973
120 END
*
```

Results

BATCH NO.	WEIGHT (KG)	
4671	.987	REJECT
3918	1.012	ACCEPT
2775	1.039	ACCEPT
5161	.991	REJECT
719	1.102	ACCEPT
3127	1.009	ACCEPT
4152	1.006	ACCEPT
5163	.973	REJECT
TOTAL REJECTED: 3		
TOTAL ACCEPTED: 5		

Points to notice

● For each batch, either one total or the other is increased by 1.

Exercise 4B

Copy and complete the flow diagram and program for this problem:

1. A transport firm overhauls its trucks every 8000 miles. For each of seven trucks, the truck number (variable T), current mileage (variable M) and mileage at last overhaul (variable L) are read.

The number of miles travelled since the last overhaul (variable C, $C=M-L$) is calculated. If this is greater than or equal to 8000 miles, an overhaul is due.

The variables T, M, L and C are printed, with the message OVERHAUL DUE if necessary.

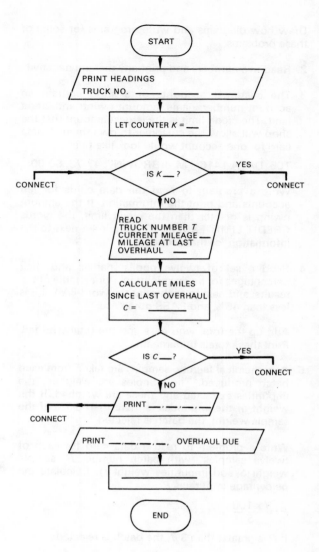

```
5 PRINT "TRUCK NO.", "_____", "_____",
                              "_____",
10 FOR K=_____ TO _____ STEP _____
15 READ T, __, __
20 LET C=_____
25 IF C _____ THEN _____
30 PRINT ___, ___, ___, ___
35 GO TO _____
40 PRINT __, __, __, __, "OVERHAUL DUE"
45 NEXT ____
50 STOP
55 _____ 7, 16715, 9133
60 DATA 5, _____, _____
65 DATA 1, _____, _____
70 DATA 6, _____, _____
75 DATA 4, _____, _____
80 DATA 2, _____, _____
85 DATA __, _____, _____
90 END
```

Draw flow diagrams and write programs for some of these problems.

2. Read five numbers and print any that are negative.

3. The customer accounts of a shop contain an account number, name, amount owing and credit limit. The credit limit is the largest amount that the shop will allow the customer to owe them. A data card for one account would look like this:

   105 DATA 1416, "M.J.BROWN", 47·73, 60·00

   Write a program to read the data cards for ten accounts and print the information. If the amount owing is greater than the credit limit, the words CREDIT LIMIT EXCEEDED are printed next to the information for that account.

4. Read a set of twelve pupils' names and their percentages for an examination. Print a table of the results, and next to each print the word FAIL if it is less than 45%, and PASS otherwise.

   Add up the total who pass and the total who fail. Print these totals underneath.

☐ 5. At a chemical factory, samples are taken from each batch produced. The samples are weighed, the impurities extracted and these are weighed. If the weight of the impurities is more than 3·7% of the sample weight, the batch is rejected.

   Write a program to read a data card for each of twelve samples (with batch number B, sample weight S and impurities weight I). Calculate the percentage impurities P:

   $$P = \frac{I \times 100}{S}$$

   If P is greater than 3·7, the batch is rejected.

   Print the input data, percentages and the message ACCEPT or REJECT as required.

   Calculate the number of batches accepted $N1$, and the number rejected $N2$. Express each number as a percentage of the number of samples.

   $$P1 = \frac{N1 \times 100}{N1 + N2}$$
   $$P2 = \frac{N2 \times 100}{N1 + N2}$$

   $P1$: percentage accepted
   $P2$: percentage rejected
   Print these percentages.

   ### Modification
   Make the program process the information for any number of samples by first reading the number of

samples from a separate data card, and using a loop of variable length.

6. Rewrite this BASIC language program, correcting the errors:

   ```
   5 PRINT THIS PROGRAM READS 10
   NUMBERS AND PRINTS THOSE GREATER
   THAN 100.
   10 FOR K FROM 1 TO 10 STEP 1
   15 READ K,
   20 IF K 100 GO TO 30
   25 GO TO 40
   30 PRINT K,
   35 K=K+1
   40 STOP
   50 END
   ```

   (University of Cambridge, Local Examinations Syndicate)

Most programs in the previous exercise can be extended to process more data by enclosing the middle part of the program in a loop.

Section 4C
Conditional calculations

Calculations must sometimes be done in different ways under different conditions, usually depending on the input data.

Example 4C1
A hired car is charged at 12p a mile for the first 100 miles, and 5p a mile for the rest, plus a fixed charge of £1.35. Write a program which reads the distance travelled, and calculates the total charge.

Method
If the mileage M is less than 100, then the formula is:

$T = ·12 + M + 1·35$

T: total charge (£) M: mileage

Otherwise, the first 100 miles costs $100 \times ·12$ and the rest $(M-100)$ costs $·05 \times (M-100)$, so the formula is:

$T = ·12 \times 100 + ·05 \times (M-100) + 1·35$

Flow diagram

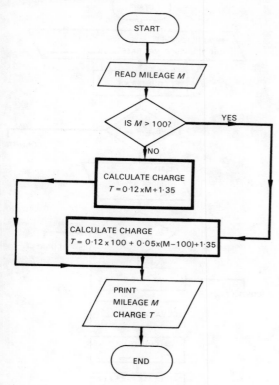

Program

```
5 READ M
10 IF M>100 THEN 25
15 LET T=0.12*M+1.35
20 GO TO 30
25 LET T=0.12*100+0.05*(M-100)+1.35
30 PRINT "MILEAGE:",M;"MILES"
35 PRINT
40 PRINT "CHARGE:","£";T
45 STOP
50 DATA 183
55 END
*
```

Results

```
MILEAGE:          183 MILES

CHARGE:           £ 17.5
```

Points to notice

● The same variable (T) is used for the total charge in statements 15 and 25.

● The print statements (30 to 40) are done whichever formula has been used to calculate T.

Example 4C2

A building materials supplier sells bricks at £4.35 per hundred to the public and at £3·94 per hundred to builders. Write a program to process five orders for bricks. Each order contains an order number, customer code (1 for the public, 2 for builders) and quantity (in hundreds of bricks). For each order, decide which price to use, and calculate the cost (cost=price × quantity). Print the order numbers, codes, quantities and costs.

Method

A loop (counter R from 1 to 5) works through the orders.

Inside the loop, the data is read. The condition:

is the customer code=1?

causes the price £4·35 to be used, otherwise the price is £3·94.

The input data and the cost are printed, and the loop continues.

Flow diagram

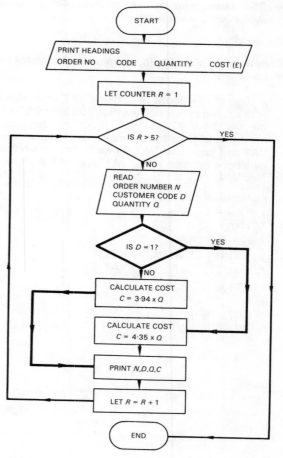

Variables

R: counter (1 to 5) N: order number
D: customer code Q: quantity
C: cost (£)

Program

```
5 PRINT "ORDER NO.","CODE","QUANTITY","COST(£)"
10 FOR R=1 TO 5 STEP 1
15 READ N,D,Q
20 IF D=1 THEN 35
25 LET C=3.94*Q
30 GO TO 40
35 LET C=4.35*Q
40 PRINT N,D,Q,C
45 NEXT R
50 STOP
55 DATA 4719,1, 4
60 DATA 2138,2,23
65 DATA 9516,2,59
70 DATA 9517,1,17
75 DATA 2139,1, 7
80 END
*
```

Results

ORDER NO.	CODE	QUANTITY	COST(£)
4719	1	4	17.4
2138	2	23	90.62
9516	2	59	232.46
9517	1	17	73.95
2139	1	7	30.45

Points to notice

● The same print statement (line 40) is used whichever price is used.

Exercise 4C

Copy and complete the flow diagram and program for this problem.

1. A shop stocks goods of different VAT rates. Items with catalogue number less than 100 have 8% VAT, the rest have 12·5% VAT. Read the catalogue number and price for ten items, and calculate the VAT and price plus VAT for each. Print a table of catalogue number, price, VAT rate, VAT and price plus VAT.

   Formulae

   $$V = \frac{R \times P}{100}$$
   $$T = V + P$$

   V: VAT (£) R: VAT rate (%)
   P: price (£) T: price+VAT (£)

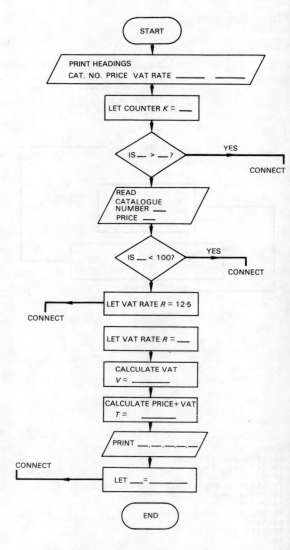

```
 5 PRINT  "CAT.  NO.",  "PRICE",  "VAT
          RATE", "_____", "_____
10 FOR K=_____ TO _____ STEP ____
15 READ ____, ____
20 IF _____ 100 THEN ____
25 LET R=12·5
30 GO TO ____
35 LET R=_____
40 LET V=_____
45 LET T=_____
50 PRINT ___, ___, ___, ___, ___
55 NEXT ____
60 STOP
65 DATA 76, 13·28, 143, 19·47
70 DATA _____, _____, _____, _____
75 _____
80 _____
85 _____
90 END
```

Draw flow diagrams and write programs for some of these problems.

2. A shop gives a 10% discount on sales totalling more than £20. Read the prices of five items sold and calculate their total. If it is more than £20, calculate the discount, otherwise the discount is zero. Also calculate the total less discount. Print the total, the discount and the total less discount.

Formulae

$D = \cdot 1 \times T$
$L = T - D$

D: discount (£) T: total (£)
L: total less discount (£)

3. Workers are paid at ordinary rate for the first 40 hours worked per week, and at overtime rate for the rest. For each of ten employees, read a name, works number, ordinary rate, overtime rate and hours worked. Calculate each worker's wage, and print a table of all the input information and the wages.

Formulae

For no overtime:
$W = R \times H$

With overtime:
$W = 40 \times R + V \times (H - 40)$

W: wage (£) R: ordinary rate (£ per hour)
H: hours worked V: overtime rate (£ per hour)

4. A plumber charges £3·25 per hour for his working time, plus a materials charge, with a minimum of £20 for each job. Write a program to read the job number, materials charge and hours worked for five jobs, in each case working out the total charge, and making it £20 where necessary.

Formula

$C = H \times 3 \cdot 25 + M$

Variables

C: charge (£) H: hours
M: materials charge (£) J: job number

5. At a bank, a charge of 8p per transaction is made on accounts where the average balance is less than £50. For each of eight accounts, read an account number, average balance and number of transactions. If necessary, calculate the charge (charge = number of transactions × 0·08). Print all the information, and the charge where there is one.

6. Write a program to find the roots x_1 and x_2 of a quadratic equation $ax^2 + bx + c = 0$ by the formulae:

$$x_1 = \frac{-b + \sqrt{(b^2 - 4ac)}}{2a}$$
$$x_2 = \frac{-b - \sqrt{(b^2 - 4ac)}}{2a}$$

Read values of a, b and c, and test if $b^2 - 4ac$ is negative. If so there are no roots.

Section 4D
Programs with more than one condition

In many programs, more than one condition is needed. The main problem is how the different conditions are linked.

Example 4D1

An examination consists of two papers. A candidate fails if his or her percentage for either paper is less than 30%. Read the candidate number, name and two percentages for six candidates. Decide whether each has passed or failed. Print a table of the information, with the word PASS or FAIL for each candidate.

Method

If the two percentages are variables $P1$ and $P2$, the conditions are:

   is $P1$ less than 30%?
or is $P2$ less than 30%?

In either case the candidate has failed.

Flow diagram

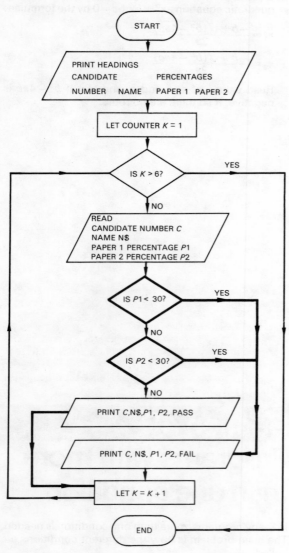

Variables

K: counter (1 to 6) C: candidate number
$N\$$: name $P1$: percentage for paper 1
$P2$: percentage for paper 2

Points to notice

● Notice carefully how the condition boxes are connected to the rest of the diagram.

Program

```
5  PRINT "CANDIDATE","PERCENTAGES"
10 PRINT "NUMBER","NAME","PAPER 1","PAPER 2"
15 PRINT
20 FOR K=1 TO 6 STEP 1
25 READ C,N$,P1,P2
30 IF P1<30 THEN 50
35 IF P2<30 THEN 50
40 PRINT C,N$,P1,P2,"PASS"
45 GO TO 55
50 PRINT C,N$,P1,P2,"FAIL"
55 NEXT K
60 STOP
65 DATA  8973,"A.JAMES    ",61,79
70 DATA  4117,"S.PENWELL  ",54,46
75 DATA  2348,"M.FEATHER  ",27,34
80 DATA  5662,"J.ADAMSON  ",58,29
85 DATA  3771,"E.STEVENS  ",43,44
90 DATA  5673,"M.HOWELL   ",19,24
95 END
```

Results

CANDIDATE NUMBER	NAME	PERCENTAGES PAPER 1	PAPER 2	
8973	A.JAMES	61	79	PASS
4117	S.PENWELL	54	46	PASS
2348	M.FEATHER	27	34	FAIL
5662	J.ADAMSON	58	29	FAIL
3771	E.STEVENS	43	44	PASS
5673	M.HOWELL	19	24	FAIL

Points to notice

● Both conditions (statements 30 and 35) lead to the same statement.

Example 4D2

A survey is conducted of the number of hours per week people spend watching television. The results are sorted into three groups:

high (more than 10 hours per week)
medium (2 to 10 hours per week)
low (less than 2 hours per week)

Write a program to read 30 such results, count the number in each group, and print these numbers.

Method

Three totals, one for each group, are first set to zero. A loop is used to work through the numbers. Two conditions are used to decide which total is increased by one:

Is the number of hours greater than 10?
This sorts out the high group.

Is the number of hours greater than or equal to 2?
This sorts out the medium group from those left.

These conditions leave one with the low group.

The three totals are printed after the loop.

Flow diagram

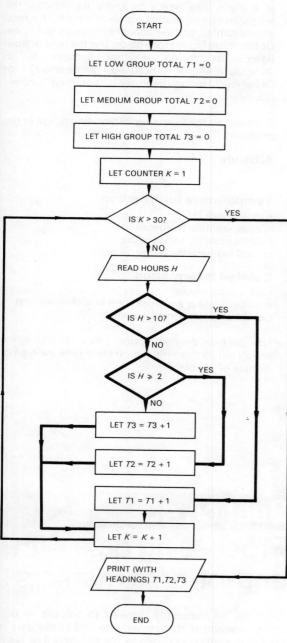

Variables

$T1$: total in low group
$T2$: total in medium group
$T3$: total in high group
K: counter (1 to 30)
H: hours watching TV per week

Program

```
5 LET T1=0
10 LET T2=0
15 LET T3=0
20 FOR K=1 TO 30 STEP 1
25 READ H
30 IF H>10 THEN 60
35 IF H>=2 THEN 50
40 LET T3=T3+1
45 GO TO 65
50 LET T2=T2+1
55 GO TO 65
60 LET T1=T1+1
65 NEXT K
70 PRINT "TV SURVEY RESULTS"
75 PRINT
80 PRINT "GROUP","HOURS PER WEEK","NUMBER OF PEOPLE"
85 PRINT
90 PRINT "HIGH","MORE THAN 10",T1
95 PRINT "MEDIUM","BETWEEN 2 AND 10",T2
100 PRINT "LOW","LESS THAN 2",T3
105 STOP
110 DATA  9, 3, 8,23, 1, 2, 7,13,19, 0
115 DATA 12, 7, 1,14,13, 4,11, 6, 5, 7
120 DATA 14, 9, 3,11, 5, 7, 8,17,21, 1
125 END
```

Results

TV SURVEY RESULTS

GROUP	HOURS PER WEEK	NUMBER OF PEOPLE
HIGH	MORE THAN 10	11
MEDIUM	BETWEEN 2 AND 10	15
LOW	LESS THAN 2	4

Exercise 4D

Copy and complete the flow diagram and program for this problem.
1. Gravel with pieces of an average length between 4 and 5 cm is required for concrete. Twelve pieces from a batch are measured. Write a program to read the twelve lengths, calculate their average and decide whether or not the batch is accepted.

Method

The conditions for rejecting the batch are:

Is the average length less than 4 cm?
or, Is the average length more than 5 cm?

Flow diagram

First draw the part of the flow diagram to calculate the average (variable A).

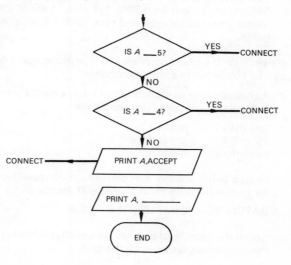

Program

Write the part to calculate the average yourself. Fill in the missing parts of the end part.

```
45 IF A _____ 5 THEN _____
50 IF A _____ 4 THEN _____
55 PRINT A, "ACCEPT"
60 GO TO _____
65 PRINT __, _____
70 STOP
75 DATA 6·1, 4·2, 5·0, 4·7, 3·8, 3·5
80 DATA _____
85 END
```

Draw flow diagrams and write programs for some of these problems:

2. Read a set of 25 numbers, and print out any in the range 10 to 20 (inclusive).

3. Read the ages of a group of 20 pupils, and count up the numbers in each of the ranges: under 13, 13 to 15, over 15.

4. Read a set of ten lengths (in metres) of beams. Print a list of these lengths, and next to each print the word REJECT if it is less than 9·98m or more than 10·02m, otherwise the word ACCEPT.

☐ 5. The examination for a subject has three papers, each out of 100 marks. To pass, a candidate must get more than 30 marks in each paper, and his total mark must be more than 100. Read in a set of sixteen results (a data card for each candidate, with a candidate number, name and three marks), calculate the total mark for each candidate, and determine whether he or she has passed or failed. Print a table of all the results, with the word PASS or FAIL next to each candidate.

☐ 6. Examination percentages are graded as follows: over 80%: grade A, 55% to 80%: grade B, 30% to 54%: grade C, less than 30%: fail. Read a set of 20 names and percentages, and print each out with its grade.

Note: With some modifications, Questions 5 and 6 can be combined in a single program.

7. A chemical is graded according to the percentage of impurities it contains. The grades are:

less than 1%:   grade 1
1% to 5%:   grade 2
more than 5%:   grade 3

Read a batch number and percentage of impurities for twelve batches. Print a table with headings:

BATCH NO.   % IMPURITIES   GRADE

Count the number of batches with each grade. Print these numbers underneath the table.

☐ 8. *Climatic classification*: To decide the type of climate at a place, one needs to know its altitude, the temperature and rainfall for each month, the total annual rainfall, and the annual average temperature. Obtain these figures for a place. Use the temperature figures to decide whether summer is in June/July/August (northern hemisphere) or December/January/February (southern hemisphere).

Then extract the following information to use in the program:

Altitude

Temperature information
annual average
hottest monthly temperature
coldest monthly temperature
annual temperature range

Rainfall information
total annual rainfall
whether there is a summer or a winter maximum
rainfall of driest summer month

Use the flow diagram opposite to write a program which inputs this information and prints the type of climate of the place.

Section 4E
Processing data with end-of-data markers

Programs are frequently required to process an unknown amount of data, where the end of the data is marked in some way (often by the numbers 0 or −1). In these cases, IF and GO TO statements are used to form a loop, which finishes when the end-of-data marker (sometimes called a *rogue value*) is reached.

Example 4E1

Read a set of numbers and find their average. It is not known how many numbers are in the set, but the end of the set is marked with the number −1, which is not part of the set.

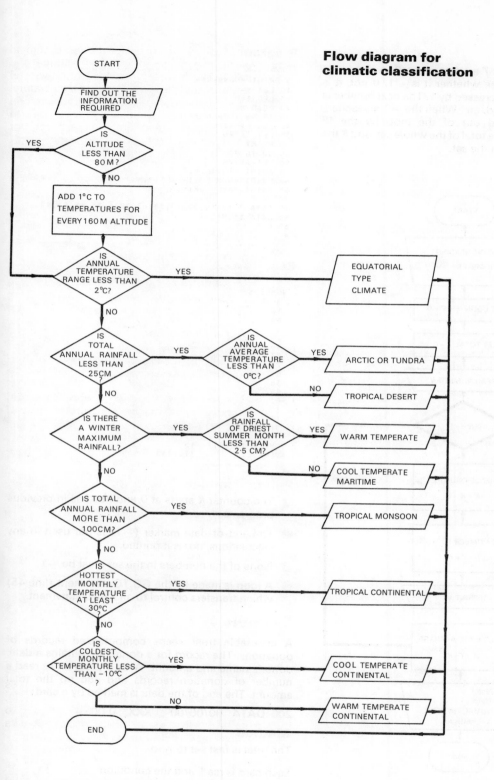

Flow diagram for climatic classification

START

FIND OUT THE INFORMATION REQUIRED

IS ALTITUDE LESS THAN 80 M? — YES

NO

ADD 1°C TO TEMPERATURES FOR EVERY 160 M ALTITUDE

IS ANNUAL TEMPERATURE RANGE LESS THAN 2°C? — YES → EQUATORIAL TYPE CLIMATE

NO

IS TOTAL ANNUAL RAINFALL LESS THAN 25CM? — YES → IS ANNUAL AVERAGE TEMPERATURE LESS THAN 0°C? — YES → ARCTIC OR TUNDRA

NO → TROPICAL DESERT

NO

IS THERE A WINTER MAXIMUM RAINFALL? — YES → IS RAINFALL OF DRIEST SUMMER MONTH LESS THAN 2·5 CM? — YES → WARM TEMPERATE

NO → COOL TEMPERATE MARITIME

NO

IS TOTAL ANNUAL RAINFALL MORE THAN 100CM? — YES → TROPICAL MONSOON

NO

IS HOTTEST MONTHLY TEMPERATURE AT LEAST 30°C? — YES → TROPICAL CONTINENTAL

NO

IS COLDEST MONTHLY TEMPERATURE LESS THAN –10°C? — YES → COOL TEMPERATE CONTINENTAL

NO → WARM TEMPERATE CONTINENTAL

END

Method

A counter K and total T are first set to 0. A number is read, and tested to see whether it is −1. If not, it is added to T and K is increased by 1. The next number is then read in and tested, etc. When the −1 is reached, control is transferred out of the loop by the IF statement. T is now the total of the whole set, and K the number of numbers in the set.

Flow diagram

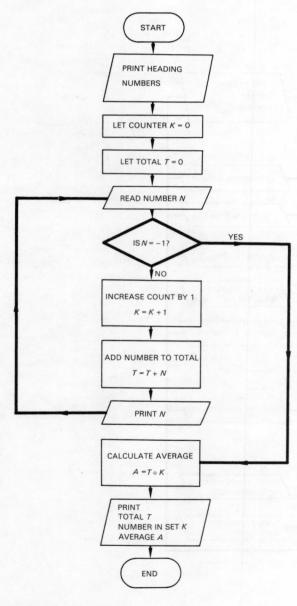

Variables

K: counter T: running total
N: each number in turn A: average

Program

```
5 PRINT "NUMBERS"
10 LET K=0
15 LET T=0
20 READ N
25 IF N=-1 THEN 50
30 LET K=K+1
35 LET T=T+N
40 PRINT N
45 GO TO 20
50 LET A=T/K
55 PRINT "TOTAL:",T
60 PRINT "NUMBER IN SET:",K
65 PRINT "AVERAGE:",A
70 STOP
75 DATA 3,18,56,23,19,48,67,22,5,36,49,63,42
80 DATA 15,91,-1
85 END
*
```

Results

```
NUMBERS
 3
 18
 56
 23
 19
 48
 67
 22
 5
 36
 49
 63
 42
 15
 91
TOTAL:            557
NUMBER IN SET:    15
AVERAGE:          37.1333
```

Points to notice

● The counter K starts at 0, and not 1 as in previous programs.

● The end-of-data marker (−1) is not used in any calculations, nor is it printed.

● None of the numbers in the set must be −1.

● A loop is made by the GO TO statement (line 45) which transfers control to an earlier statement.

Example 4E2

A charitable trust keeps computerized records of donations. The record for a donation contains a date, donor's name and amount. Write a program to read a number of donation records and add up the total amount. The end of the data is marked by a card:

200 DATA "00/00/00", "XXX", 0·00

Method

The total is first set to zero.

Each card is read, and the condition

Is the date 00/00/00?

tests if the end of the data has been reached. If not, the amount is added to the total, and the next card read.

Flow diagram

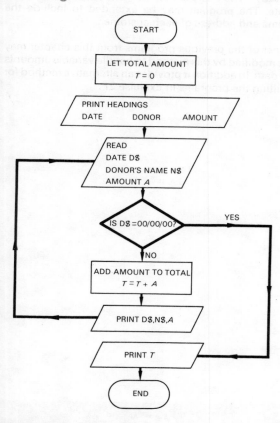

Variables

T: total (£) $D\$$: date $N\$$: name
A: amount (£)

Program

```
 5 LET T=0
10 PRINT "DATE","DONOR","AMOUNT (£)"
12 PRINT
15 READ D$,N$,A
20 IF D$="00/00/00"THEN 40
25 LET T=T+A
30 PRINT D$,N$,A
35 GO TO 15
40 PRINT ,"TOTAL",T
45 DATA "27/11/75","A.M.BOWLES  ",1500.00
50 DATA "03/02/76","K.M.SMITH   ", 472.75
55 DATA "18/02/76","A.FREDERICKS",  33.41
60 DATA "27/03/76","J.BARNES    ", 149.73
65 DATA "06/04/76","P.METCALF   ",2160.00
70 DATA "00/00/00","XXX         ",   0.00
75 END
*
```

Results

DATE	DONOR	AMOUNT (£)
27/11/75	A.M.BOWLES	1500
03/02/76	K.M.SMITH	472.75
18/02/76	A.FREDERICKS	33.41
27/03/76	J.BARNES	149.73
06/04/76	P.METCALF	2160
	TOTAL	4315.89

Points to notice

● The first comma in line 40 is used to put the total in the correct column.

Exercise 4E

Copy and complete the flow diagram and program for this problem:

1. A certain kind of fencing requires 345 posts and 4·2 km of wire for every kilometre of fence. Read the contract numbers and lengths for a number of contracts. For each, calculate the number of posts and length of wire required. Use an end-of-data marker with contract number zero.

Formulae

$N = 345 \times L$
$W = 4 \cdot 2 \times L$

N: number of posts L: length of fence (km)
W: length of wire (km) C: contract number

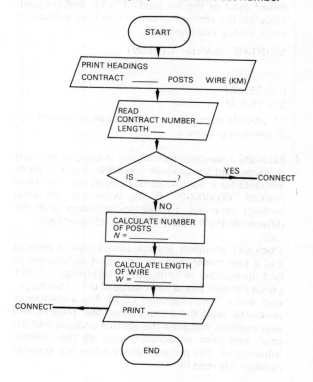

```
    5 PRINT "CONTRACT", _____, "POSTS",
                                 WIRE (KM)"
   10 READ ____, ____
   15 IF _____ THEN ____
   20 LET N=_____
   25 LET W=_____
   30 PRINT ____, ____, ____, ____
   35 _____
   40 STOP
   45 DATA 417, 93
   50 _____
   ...
  ____ DATA ____, ____
  ____ END
```

Draw flow diagrams and write programs for some of these problems. The last data item must be an end-of-data marker.

2. Make a list of a number of authors and titles of books. Put this information in data statements (one author and title per statement). Mark the end of the list with the statement

   150 DATA "AAA", "BBB"

   Write a program to read this information and print a list of it.

3. 1 kg of mortar requires $\frac{1}{4}$ kg of cement and $\frac{3}{4}$ kg of sand. Read a number of amounts of mortar to be mixed (end of the list marked -1), and for each calculate the amount of cement and the amount of sand. Print a table headed:

   MORTAR SAND CEMENT

   Formulae

   $C = \cdot 25 \times M$
   $S = \cdot 75 \times M$

   M: amount of mortar C: amount of cement
   S: amount of sand

4. Each day a company records the amount of money it receives, and the amount it spends. Read in these amounts for a number of days, with the date (end marked "00/00/00", 0, 0), work out the total amount received, total amount spent and the difference. Print a table of all the information.

☐ 5. Electricity accounts are calculated from a present and a past meter reading. These are subtracted to find the number of units used. The charge is 1·841 pence per unit, plus a fuel charge of 0·112 pence per unit, and a fixed charge of £2.21. For a number of accounts, read the account number, present and past reading, calculate the various charges and the total, and print an account with all the relevant information. The program stops when the account number 0 is read in.

Note: The charges may be altered if they are out of date. The program may be extended to include the name and address of each customer.

Most of the previous programs from this chapter may be modified by this method to handle variable amounts of data. In addition it provides an alternative method for writing the programs in Exercise 2F.

Section 4F
Using conditions to end loops

In many cases a calculation must be performed repeatedly until some quantity passes a certain size. A condition tests this quantity to see whether the loop continues.

Example 4F

The motor car production of a country in 1975 was 432 561. If it increases at 5% per year, when will it first exceed 1 000 000 cars?

Method

A 5% increase means that each year's production is 1·05 times the previous year's production. A variable T (time) is first set to 1975, and a variable P (production) to 432 561. Then T is increased by 1, and P multiplied by 1·05. If P is now less than 1 000 000, P and T are again increased. If P has passed 1 000 000 the loop is ended.

Flow diagram

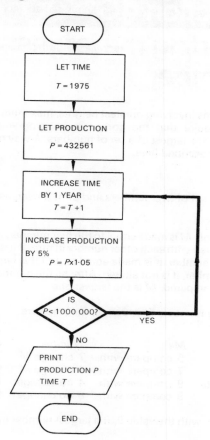

Variables

T: time (year AD)
P: production (cars per year)

Program

```
 5 LET T=1975
10 LET P=432561
15 LET T=T+1
20 LET P=P*1.05
25 IF P<1000000 THEN 15
30 PRINT "PRODUCTION FIRST EXCEEDS 1000000 IN ";T
35 PRINT "WHEN PRODUCTION IS ";P;" CARS"
40 STOP
45 END
*
```

Results

```
PRODUCTION FIRST EXCEEDS 1000000 IN   1993
WHEN PRODUCTION IS  1.04101E6  CARS
```

Points to notice

- There must be no commas or spaces in the long numbers in statements 10 and 25.

- The conditions IF P=1000000 ... or IF P><1000000 ... must *not* be used, as P may pass this value without actually being equal to it.
- Care must be taken to avoid putting the computer into an endless loop with this type of program.

Exercise 4F

Copy and complete the flow diagram and program for this problem:

1. The height of a certain type of tree after a number of years is calculated by the formula

$$H = 14 \cdot 2 - \frac{14 \cdot 2}{T+1}$$

T: time (years) H: height (metres)

In what year will its height first exceed 10 metres?

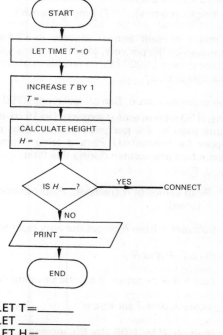

```
 5 LET T=_____
10 LET _____
15 LET H=_____
20 IF H _____ THEN _____
25 PRINT "_____", ____, "YEARS"
30 _____
35 END
```

Draw flow diagrams and write programs for some of these problems:

2. The population of Kuwait was 0·7 million in 1970. If it increases at 8·3% per year, in what year will it pass 5 million?

3. A radioactive substance halves its activity every ten days. If its present activity is 1000 emissions per second, after how long (to the nearest ten days) will it drop below 1 emission per second?

4. A train travelling at 50 metres per second slows down by 2 metres per second every second. Print a table of time (at 1 second intervals), speed and distance (from where it started slowing down) until it has stopped.

   distance travelled during each 1 second interval
   =(speed in the middle of that interval)×1 second
   =(speed at the beginning of the interval−1 metre per second)×1 second

5. A ball is thrown upwards at 15 metres per second. Print a table of heights at different times (at 0·2 second intervals) until it again reaches the ground.

   $H=15 \times T-4 \cdot 9 \times T^2$

   H: height (metres) T: time (seconds)

6. A man's present annual income is £3000. If it increases by 5% per year, after how many years will it have passed £5000? What will his total income be over this period?

7. The estimated North Sea oil reserve is 2290 million tons. If 20 million tons is extracted in 1976, and this figure rises by 6% per year, in what year will the supply be exhausted? Print a table of the year, production and reserve during this time.

   ### Method

   ● Read values of R (reserve), P (production) and T (time).

   1. Subtract P from R to get the new reserve

   2. Print T, P and R

   3. Test if R is negative. If so, the program ends

   4. Increase time T by 1 year

   5. Multiply P by 1·06 (for 6% increase) to get the new production level

   6. Go back to step 1

   ### Modifications

   ● Use percentages other than 6% and see what difference they make to the time taken to exhaust the reserve.

   ● Programs like this can be used for many situations where resources are being used up at an increasing rate.

Section 4G
Finding the largest number

Problems involving greatest heights, maximum profits, etc. require that the computer be programmed to choose the largest of a set of numbers. A way of doing this is described here.

Example 4G1

Read a set of five numbers and print the largest one.

Method

A variable M is made equal to the first number. It is then compared with each other number in turn. If it is smaller than a number, it is made equal to it. If it is larger than the number, it is not altered. After all the numbers have been compared, M is the largest one.

For the numbers 5, 7, 9, 4, 8, the steps are:

	M		Number		New value of M
start:	5	compare with:	7	change M:	7
M from	7	compare with:	9	change M:	9
previous	9	compare with:	4	no change:	9
line:	9	compare with:	8	no change:	9

M ends with the value 9, the largest number in the set

Flow diagram

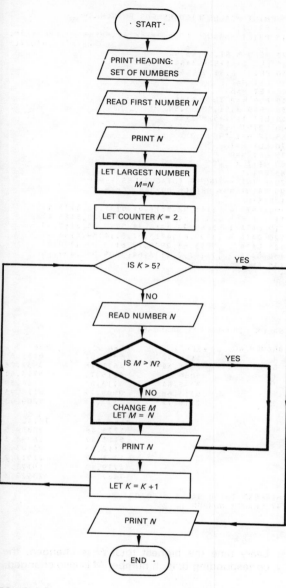

Variables

M: largest number   K: counter (2 to 5)
N: number in the set

Program

```
5 PRINT "SET OF NUMBERS"
10 PRINT
15 READ N
20 LET M=N
25 PRINT N
30 FOR K=2 TO 5 STEP 1
35 READ N
40 IF M>N THEN 50
45 LET M=N
50 PRINT N
55 NEXT K
60 PRINT
65 PRINT "LARGEST NUMBER",M
70 STOP
75 DATA 5,7,9,4,8
80 END
*
```

Results

```
SET OF NUMBERS

  5
  7
  9
  4
  8

LARGEST NUMBER   9
```

Points to notice

● The loop counter must start at 2, since the first number is read before the loop starts.

● The condition (line 40) is the one for not changing M. This shortens the program.

Example 4G2 □

A firm has six branches. At the end of each month, a data card is prepared for each branch with the branch number and four sales figures. Write a program to read these cards, work out the total sales for each branch and print a table headed:

BRANCH NO.   WEEK 1   WEEK 2   WEEK 3
                               WEEK 4   TOTAL

Also print the highest total sale, and the branch having that total.

Method

In addition to a variable for the current highest total sales (variable H), there must be one for the corresponding branch number (variable M). The headings are printed, the first data card read and the total sales for that branch calculated. Variable H is made equal to this total, and variable M to the branch number.

A loop is used to read the other data cards, add up the total sales for each branch and compare this total with H. If H is larger than the total, no change is made. Otherwise H is made equal to the total and M to the corresponding branch number.

Numbers in the table are printed before and during the loop. The highest total and corresponding branch number are printed afterwards.

Flow diagram

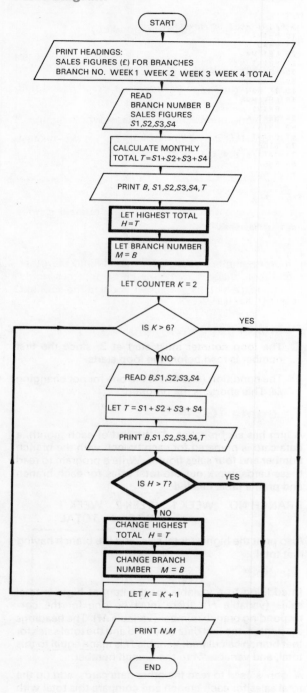

START

PRINT HEADINGS:
SALES FIGURES (£) FOR BRANCHES
BRANCH NO. WEEK1 WEEK 2 WEEK 3 WEEK 4 TOTAL

READ
BRANCH NUMBER B
SALES FIGURES
S1,S2,S3,S4

CALCULATE MONTHLY
TOTAL T=S1+S2+S3+S4

PRINT B, S1,S2,S3,S4,T

LET HIGHEST TOTAL
H=T

LET BRANCH NUMBER
M=B

LET COUNTER K=2

IS K > 6? —— YES

NO

READ B,S1,S2,S3,S4

LET T = S1 + S2 + S3 + S4

PRINT B,S1,S2,S3,S4,T

IS H > T? —— YES

NO

CHANGE HIGHEST
TOTAL H = T

CHANGE BRANCH
NUMBER M = B

LET K = K + 1

PRINT N,M

END

Variables

B: branch number   K: counter (2 to 6)
S1, S2, S3, S4: sales (£) for the four weeks
T: total sales (£)   H: highest total (£)
M: branch number with highest total

Program

```
5 PRINT "SALES FIGURES FOR BRANCHES"
10 PRINT
15 PRINT "BRANCH NO.","WEEK 1","WEEK 2","WEEK 3",
                                 "WEEK 4","TOTAL"
20 READ B,S1,S2,S3,S4
25 LET T=S1+S2+S3+S4
30 PRINT B,S1,S2,S3,S4,T
35 LET H=T
40 LET M=B
45 FOR K=2 TO 6 STEP 1
50 READ B,S1,S2,S3,S4
55 LET T=S1+S2+S3+S4
60 PRINT B,S1,S2,S3,S4,T
65 IF H>T THEN 80
70 LET H=T
75 LET M=B
80 NEXT K
85 PRINT
90 PRINT "HIGHEST TOTAL SALES : ";H
95 PRINT "BY BRANCH NUMBER : ";B
100 STOP
105 DATA 4 ,4116.92,5817.61,6131.50,4773.48
110 DATA 6 ,2971.34,4871.16,3937.28,5113.47
115 DATA 1 ,5060.90,4216.74,5713.94,8112.35
120 DATA 5 ,3895.64,4713.87,8114.39,4793.27
125 DATA 3 ,5313.68,2909.72,6118.93,4779.43
130 DATA 2 ,7116.72,4173.64,5209.03,7427.94
135 END
*
```

Results

```
SALES FIGURES FOR BRANCHES

BRANCH NO.     WEEK 1          WEEK 2          WEEK 3
4              4116.92         5817.61         6131.5
6              2971.34         4871.16         3937.28
1              5060.9          4216.74         5713.94
5              3895.64         4713.87         8114.39
3              5313.68         2909.72         6118.93
2              7116.72         4173.64         5209.03

               WEEK 4          TOTAL
               4773.48         20839.5
               5113.47         16893.3
               8112.35         23103.9
               4793.27         21517.2
               4779.43         19121.8
               7427.94         23927.3

HIGHEST TOTAL SALES :   23927.3
BY BRANCH NUMBER :    2
```

Points to notice

● Every time the highest total H is changed, the corresponding branch number M is also changed.

Exercise 4G

Draw flow diagrams and write programs for some of these problems. Some will need RESTORE statements and the data to be read twice.

1. Read a set of numbers and print the smallest one.

2. Read a set of numbers (of unknown length, end marked by −1), and print the largest one.

☐ 3. Read a set of 20 numbers. Find the largest, the smallest and the difference between them.

4. Find the smallest of a set of 16 numbers. Print a table with each number and the amount by which it is greater than the smallest number.

5. Calculate the average of a set of numbers. Then find the number which is closest to the average. (Because the numbers are above and below the average, consider the square of the difference between a number and the average: $d=(n-a)^2$, d: square difference, n: number, a: average. The number for which this difference is the smallest is the required number.)

6. The height of a rocket a certain number of seconds after launching is:

$$h=1550t-5t^2$$

h: height (metres) t: time (seconds)

Calculate the height each second after launch until it lands again, printing only the maximum height and the time to reach this height.

7. At a shop, the price of tins of fruit was varied to see which price gave the maximum income. A record was kept of the price and the number sold per week.

Price (pence)	Number sold
10	879
11	835
11·5	794
12	732
13	587
15	463

Write a program to read this information and calculate the income (income=number sold × price) at each price. Print a table of price, number sold and income. Find the maximum income, and the price at which it occurred. Print these below the table.

Section 4H
Whole numbers only

A computer can be instructed to take the whole number part of a number by the word INT (short for INTEGER).

For example:

INT (3·3)   =3
INT (2·9985) =2 (it does not round up)
INT (5)   =5

This has several uses:

● To see whether numbers divide exactly (and find factors).

● Rounding numbers to the nearest whole number.

● Approximating sums of money to the nearest penny. An example is given of each use.

Example 4H1

Write a program to test whether one number divides exactly into another.

Method

If the one number does divide exactly into the other, then the quotient is a whole number. In other words, the integer part of the quotient is equal to the quotient.

Flow diagram

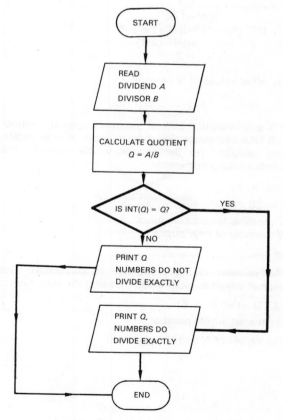

Variables

A: dividend B: divisor Q: quotient

Program

```
5 READ A,B
10 PRINT "IS ";A;" / ";B;" EXACT ?"
15 LET Q=A/B
20 IF INT(Q)=Q THEN 35
25 PRINT "ANSWER:",Q,"NOT EXACT"
30 GO TO 40
35 PRINT "ANSWER:",Q,"EXACT"
40 STOP
45 DATA 31742,149
50 END
*
```

Results

```
IS 31742 / 149 EXACT ?
ANSWER:         213.034      NOT EXACT
```

Rounding to the nearest whole number is done by adding ·5 to a number and then taking the whole number part.

INT $(N+·5)$ gives the nearest whole number to N

For example, if $N=1·2$,
$$INT (N+·5) = INT (1·2+·5)$$
$$= INT (1·7)$$
$$= \underline{1}$$
if $N=1·6$,
$$INT (N+·5) = INT (1·6+·5)$$
$$= INT (2·1)$$
$$= \underline{2}$$

Try other values of N yourself.

Example 4H2

It is estimated that 28% of the new pupils at a school will take commerce. Read the number of new pupils, and calculate (to the nearest whole number) the number taking commerce.

Formula

$C=·28 \times N$

C: number taking commerce
N: number of new pupils

Method

The number taking commerce is calculated. The nearest whole number is found, using the statement:

LET $D=INT (C+·5)$
D: nearest whole number

The values of N and D are printed.

Flow diagram

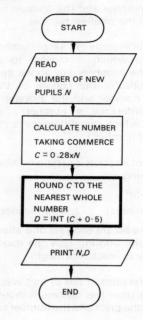

Program

```
5 READ N
10 LET C=.28*N
15 LET D=INT(C+.5)
20 PRINT "NUMBER OF NEW PUPILS : ";N
25 PRINT "NUMBER TAKING COMMERCE : ";D
30 STOP
35 DATA 258
40 END
*
```

Results

```
NUMBER OF NEW PUPILS :   258
NUMBER TAKING COMMERCE :  72
```

The nearest penny

Calculations frequently give sums of money containing fractions of a penny, such as £48·3781 for 48 pounds 37·81 pence. Amounts like this can be rounded to the nearest penny by

● multiplying the amount by 100

● adding ·5

● taking the whole number part

● dividing by 100.

INT $(100*A+·5)/100$

rounds the amount A to the nearest penny.

Example 4H3

If $A = 48 \cdot 3781$, INT $(100*A + \cdot 5)/100$
$= $INT $(100 \times 48 \cdot 3781 + \cdot 5)/100$
$= $INT $(4837 \cdot 81 + \cdot 5)/100$
$= $INT $(4838 \cdot 31)/100$
$= \qquad 4838/100$
$= \qquad \underline{48 \cdot 38}$

Try other amounts yourself.

Example 4H4

On 4th July 1976 the exchange rate for pounds to dollars was £1 = \$1·776. Read an amount in dollars, and convert it to pounds (to the nearest penny) at this exchange rate.

Method

For every \$1·776, £1 is exchanged. The dollars must be divided by 1·776 to get the pounds.

$P = D \div 1 \cdot 776$

P: pounds D: dollars

The pounds are then rounded to the nearest penny by the method shown:

$R = $ INT $(100*P + \cdot 5)/100$

R: pounds (to the nearest penny)

Flow diagram

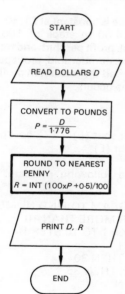

Program

```
5 READ D
10 LET P=D/1.776
15 LET R=INT(100*P+.5)/100
20 PRINT "$";D;" CONVERTS TO £";R
25 STOP
30 DATA 134.47
35 END
*
```

Results

```
$ 134.47   CONVERTS TO £ 75.72
```

Exercise 4H

Draw flow diagrams and write programs for some of these problems.

1. Read a set of ten numbers and test whether each is even or odd (an even number gives a whole number when divided by 2).

☐ 2. Work out how a given sum of money can be made up in the least number of notes and coins. If the money (m) is read in with a decimal point separating pounds and pence, then:

   number of £5 notes $= $ INT $(m/5)$

   Subtract the sum of money this represents from the original sum, and then find the number of £1 notes, etc.

3. A shop receives packaged food in boxes, each box containing a number of packets. Read reference numbers, box prices and numbers of packets for ten boxes. Calculate the price per packet for each box. Round this price to the nearest penny.

$$P = \frac{B}{N}$$

P: price per packet (£) B: price of a box (£)
N: number of packets in a box

Print a table of all the information.

4. The profits of a company are divided amongst its shareholders. Read the profits and the number of shareholders. Calculate the dividend (the profit per share) correct to the nearest penny.

$$D = \frac{P}{N}$$

D: dividend (£) P: profit (£)
N: number of shareholders

5. An earthmoving contractor has lorries which can carry 5175 kg. Read a list of amounts of earth to be moved, and in each case calculate the number of lorry loads required.

6. A number is a factor of another number if it divides into it exactly. Write a program which reads in a number, then prints a list of its factors.

(Try all the numbers from 2 to half the input number and see if they divide exactly.)

☐ 7. A number is prime if it has no factors other than one and itself. Write a program (or modify the one from Question 6) to read a set of numbers and test whether each is prime.

☐ 8. Write a program (based on the one from Question 7) to print a list of all the prime numbers up to 100.

☐ 9. Insulating material is sold in rolls measuring 10 m by ·5 m. Read the length and breadth of a number of surfaces to be insulated, and calculate the area of each. Calculate the total area, add 5% for wastage and then calculate the number of rolls required.

Exercise 4I
These problems revise methods introduced in this chapter.

1. Write a list of some places of interest to visit in your vicinity.

Write a program to read this information from data cards, and print it, stopping when the last card (with the words END OF LIST) is reached.

2. Passengers are allowed up to 20 kg of luggage on an aeroplane. Prepare data cards for five passengers, each with a name and the weights of three luggage items. Put zeros for passengers with less than three items.

Read this information, calculate the total weight for each passenger. Print a list of passengers' names and total luggage weights, with the message OVERWEIGHT if necessary.

3. At a farm, records are kept of the number of eggs produced each day. A record contains the date and the number of small, medium and large eggs produced that day.

Read a number of these records from data cards (last card marked "∗∗∗", 0, 0, 0). Calculate the total small, total medium and total large eggs produced. Print a table of all the information and the totals.

4. The population of India was 554·6 millions in 1970, increasing at 2·6% per year. Print a table of the population each year until it reaches 1000 millions.

5. The equation $x^3 + x = 11$ has a solution slightly greater than 2 (if $x=2$, $x^3+x=10$). Find this solution to two decimal places by calculating $y = x^3 + x$ for values of x increasing in steps of 0·0 from $x=2$, stopping when y first exceeds 11.

☐ 6. The lengths of a set of metal parts (in millimetres are read, with the end marked by −1. A part is to b rejected if its length differs by more than 0·1 mr from the average, i.e. if the difference is greate than 0·1 or less than −0·1. Calculate the averag length, then print a table of the lengths an differences, with the word REJECT where ne cessary.

☐ 7. A number of loaves of bread are taken from bakery production line and weighed (in kilograms to three decimal places). Read these weight (end marked 0), calculate the average and th range (largest minus smallest). Express the rang as a percentage of the average.

$$P = \frac{R \times 100}{A}$$

P: percentage   R: range   A: average

☐ 8. The number of shirts sold per month by a chain o shops is related to the price of the shirts by th formula

$$N = 10000 - 2000 \times P$$

N: number sold per month   P: price (£)

The cost price is constant at £1·60. For prices fron £2·00 to £4·00 in steps of 10p, calculate th number sold, profit per shirt, and total profit. Print table of price, number sold, profit per shirt and tota profit. Also find the maximum profit, and the pric at which this occurs.

$$R = P - C$$
$$T = N \times R$$

R: profit per shirt (£)   C: cost price (=£1·60)
T: total profit (£)

9. Rewrite the following program, correcting th mistakes.

```
REM PROGRAM TO FIND NUMBERS LESS
THAN 5 OR MORE THAN 10.
  5 FOR KK=1 TO 10 STEP 1
 10 READ N,
 10 IF N 5, THEN 30
 20 IF N 10, THEN 35
 30 PRINT N,
 35 NEXT N.
 40 STOP
 45 DATA 7, −11, ·4, 8, 40,
 50 END
```

10. Write a BASIC program to input a list of 40 examination marks and output the list with FAIL PASS or DISTINCTION alongside each mark

Output FAIL, if the mark is less than 50, PASS if the mark is between 50 and 60 inclusive, and DISTINCTION if the mark is 70 or over.

(East Anglian Examinations Board)

1. Simplify the following BASIC program without altering the results produced. You may use any BASIC instructions or techniques you know to achieve this.

```
10 LET C1=1
20 LET C2=1
30 LET T=0
40 INPUT M
50 LET T=T+M
60 IF C2>=5 THEN 90
70 LET C2=C2+1
80 GO TO 40
90 PRINT T
100 IF C1>=20 THEN 130
110 LET C1=C1+1
120 GO TO 20
130 END
```

(East Anglian Examinations Board)

2. The BASIC program shown below is supposed to find the largest of 50 numbers, which are to be supplied as data. It inputs the first number into L and then compares each successive number (X) with the value of L. If any number is found to be greater than L, then L is replaced by it.

```
10 FOR N=1 TO 50
20 INPUT L
30 INPUT X
40 IF L>=X THEN 60
50 X=L
60 NEXT N
70 END
```

The program as shown has four faults in it. Three of these are logical errors such that the program will not work properly. The fourth error is the omission of a necessary instruction. You may assume that all the statements shown are valid BASIC statements.

(a) Find the three logical errors and say why each would have caused the program to go wrong.
(b) Say what statement is missing.
(c) Write out a correct version of the program.

(East Anglian Examinations Board)

3. Write a program in BASIC which will select and output the largest and smallest numbers from a list of positive numbers terminating with a negative rogue value. Start by drawing a flowchart.

(East Anglian Examinations Board)

4. Given that $y=x^3+5x$ draw a flowchart and use it to write a BASIC program to produce a TABLE, with HEADINGS, of the value of x and y. The

values of x are to start at 1 and increase by 1 at a time until the program terminates when $y>50000$.

(East Anglian Examinations Board)

15. Document a program which works out the average mark obtained by candidates in a history examination using the following information:

(a) The data for each candidate consists of .a unique number followed by a mark (max. 100).
(b) A pass is obtained if the mark is 50 or over, and a distinction if the mark is 80 or over.
(c) Output

(i) the candidate's number, mark and whether he failed, passed, passed with distinction
(ii) the total number of failures, passes, distinctions

Code your program in a suitable language.

(Welsh Joint Education Committee)

16. Dry run the flowchart below, putting the output on the line indicated. Now write a BASIC program from this flowchart on the coding sheet provided.

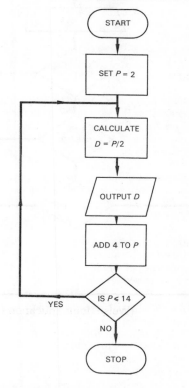

The numbers output will be ————————

(East Anglian Examinations Board)

75

17. In a biology experiment to find out how many pupils' eyes were blue or brown, a random sample of about a hundred was taken and the information (E) coded as

0 for blue eyes,
1 for brown eyes,
2 for other colours.

The information is terminated by −1.

Program the following flowchart to process the information.

to find the number of pupils with blue or brown eyes

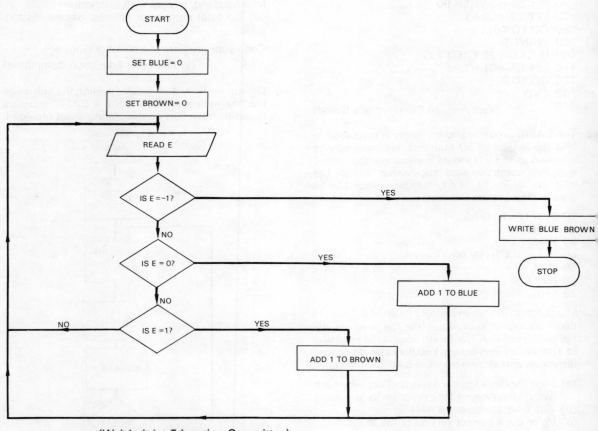

(Welsh Joint Education Committee)

18. The examination marks of Peter Jones are as follows:

English	58	Science	45
Mathematics	52	Art	37
Geography	61	Craft	72
History	48	Woodwork	83

To pass an examination, Peter must obtain at least 45 marks. A Credit is given for any subject with a mark above 70.

Draw a flowchart and write a program using a high-level language to show the grades obtained by Peter in each subject (i.e. Credit, Pass or Fail). Your output should be suitable for the completion of the RESULT column on a pre-printed form like the one shown below.

SUBJECT	RESULT
English	
Mathematics	
Geography	
History	
Science	
Art	
Craft	
Woodwork	

(Yorkshire Regional Examinations Board)

19. A year is a leap year if it is divisible by 4, except that a century year is only a leap year if it is divisible by 400.

(a) Draw a flow diagram to show how to determine whether a particular year is a leap year, and to start "_____ is a leap year" or "_____ is not a leap year".

(b) Apply a "dry run" to your flow chart for the year 1900.

(c) Using a high-level programming language, write a program to enable the instructions in your flow diagram to be carried out on a computer.

(Yorkshire Regional Examinations Board)

5. Interactive programs

All the programs in this book can be run on a micro-computer or a terminal, but programs which require information to be supplied during their actual running cannot be run in any other way. These include games and simulating activities like driving a car.

Flow diagram

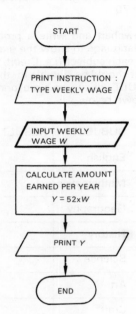

Section 5A
The INPUT statement

This is a way of supplying information to a program while it is actually running. It works like a READ statement, except that there is no accompanying DATA statement. When the computer reaches the INPUT statement, a request to type appears on the terminal or microcomputer display screen. The required information is then typed, as if it was in a DATA statement, and the program continues.

Example 5A1

Input a person's weekly wage and calculate how much he or she earns in a year.

$Y = 52 \times W$

Y: amount earned in a year (£)
W: weekly wage (£)

Program

```
 5 PRINT "TYPE WEEKLY WAGE"
10 INPUT W
15 LET Y= 52*W
20 PRINT "AMOUNT EARNED PER YEAR:",Y
25 STOP
30 END
```

Results

```
TYPE WEEKLY WAGE
   43.52
AMOUNT EARNED PER YEAR 2263.04
STOPPED AT LINE 25
```

Points to notice

● There is no DATA statement. The data number i supplied while the program is running.

Example 5A2

Write a program to estimate the number of litres of paint needed to paint a room. The information required during the running of the program is:

- the number of walls to be painted
- the length and height of each wall (in metres)
- the number of square metres covered by one litre of paint

Method

The total area to be painted (variable T) is calculated.

A loop is used (of variable length N, the number of walls) in which a length and a height (variables L and H) are input, and the area of the wall (variable A) calculated.

$A = L \times H$

The area is added to the total.

After the loop, the number of square metres covered by one litre of paint (variable C) is input, and the number of litres of paint (variable L) calculated.

$$L = \frac{T}{C}$$

The total area and number of litres required are printed.

An instruction is printed before each piece of information is required.

Flow diagram

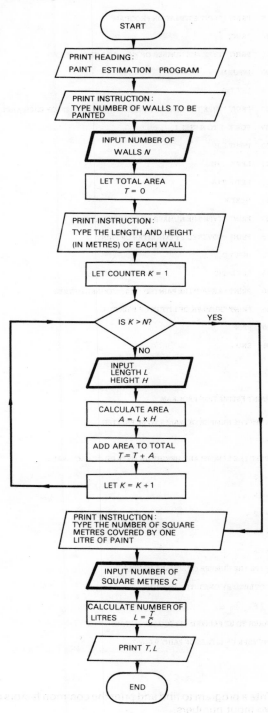

79

Program

```
 5   PRINT "PAINT ESTIMATION PROGRAM"

10   PRINT

15   PRINT "TYPE THE NUMBER OF WALLS TO BE PAINTED"

20   INPUT N

25   LET T=0

30   PRINT "TYPE THE LENGTH AND HEIGHT (IN METRES) OF EACH WALL"

35   FOR K=1 TO N STEP 1

40   INPUT L,H

45   LET A=L*H

50   LET T=T+A

55   NEXT K

60   PRINT "TYPE THE NUMBER OF SQUARE METRES"

65   PRINT "COVERED BY ONE LITRE OF PAINT"

70   INPUT C

75   LET L=T/C

80   PRINT "AREA TO BE PAINTED : "; T; "SQUARE METRES"

85   PRINT "NUMBER OF LITRES OF PAINT"; L

90   STOP

95   END
```

Results

```
PAINT ESTIMATION PROGRAM

TYPE THE NUMBER OF WALLS TO BE PAINTED

←5

TYPE THE LENGTH AND HEIGHT (IN METRES) OF EACH WALL

←4,3

←4,5

←6,2

←3,3

←5,3

TYPE THE NUMBER OF SQUARE METRES

COVERED BY ONE LITRE OF PAINT

←7.5

AREA TO BE PAINTED : 68 SQUARE METRES

NUMBER OF LITRES OF PAINT 9.06667
```

☐ Example 5A3

Write a program to find and print the common factors of two input numbers.

Method

The smaller of the two input numbers is found (variable L). Each whole number from 1 to L is tested to see if it

divides exactly into the input numbers. If it does not divide exactly, the program moves on to the next number; if it does divide exactly then it is printed. The last number printed will be the highest common factor of the two input numbers.

If one number divides exactly into another, the whole number part of the quotient will be equal to the quotient. The condition is thus

Is $A/K = \text{INT}(A/K)$?

A: input number K: test factor

Flow diagram

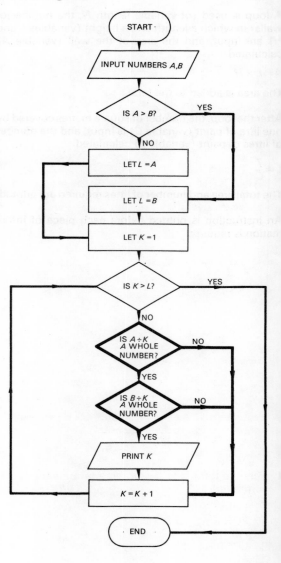

Variables

A, B: input numbers
L: smaller of A or B = limit of loop
K: numbers to be tested to see if they are factors
(counter from 1 to L)

Program

```
←  5  PRINT "TYPE IN TWO NUMBERS"
←  7  PRINT "THIS PROGRAM FINDS THEIR COMMON FACTORS"
← 10  INPUT A,B
← 15  PRINT "COMMON FACTORS OF"; A; "AND"; B
← 20  IF A > B THEN 35
← 25  LET L = A
← 30  GO TO 40
← 35  LET L = B
← 40  FOR K = 1 TO L STEP 1
← 45  IF INT (A/K) < > A/K THEN 60
← 50  IF INT (B/K) < > B/K THEN 60
← 55  PRINT K
← 60  NEXT K
← 65  STOP
← 70  END
```

Results

```
TYPE IN TWO NUMBERS

THIS PROGRAM FINDS THEIR COMMON FACTORS

← 60,20

COMMON FACTORS OF 60 AND 20

1

2

4

5

10

20

STOPPED AT LINE 65
```

Points to notice

Statement 45 means: 'If K does not divide exactly
into A then go to statement 60.'

Exercise 5A

1. This program is to be run on a terminal or micro-computer:

```
 5 PRINT "RECIPROCALS PROGRAM"
10 FOR K=1 TO 3 STEP 1
15 INPUT N
20 LET R=1/N
25 PRINT R
30 NEXT K
35 STOP
40 END
```

(a) How many input numbers will be needed?
(b) Write a set of suitable input numbers and the
results they would produce.

Draw flow diagrams and write programs for some of
these problems:

2. Input an amount of money you wish to save, and the
amount you can save per week. Calculate the
number of weeks (or months or years) it will take to
save the amount.

$$N = \frac{A}{W}$$

N: number of weeks   A: amount to be saved (£)
W: amount saved per week (£)

3. Write a program which accepts a number and works
out its multiplication table from 1 to 10. For example
if 31 is put in, then the computer prints 31, 62, 93, . . .
up to 310.

4. Input the conversion rate for a foreign currency (e.g.
£1 = 9·05 francs) and print out a conversion table to
that currency for amounts from £1 to £20.

5. Input the length of a journey, and print a table of the
times it would take at average speeds of 30 mph, 35
mph . . . up to 70 mph.

$$T = \frac{D}{S}$$

T: time (hours)   D: distance (miles)
S: speed (mph)

☐ 6. A graph is to be drawn of the equation $y = ax + b$,
where a and b are constants, and x varies from 0 to
10. Write a program to accept values of a and b as
input, and calculate y for the various values of x.
Print a table of the x and y values.

(This program may be written for quadratic equations $y = ax^2 + bx + c$, where a, b and c are input, and
x varies from −5 to 5, or other equations and other
ranges of x.)

☐ 7. Calculate the lowest common denominator of two
input numbers. Find the larger number, multiply it
by 1, 2, 3, 4 . . ., each time testing whether the
smaller number divides exactly into the product. The
first product into which it does divide exactly is the
lowest common denominator.

This process may be generalized for more than two
numbers. Find the largest input number, multiply it
by 1, 2, 3, 4 . . . each time dividing the product by all
the other input numbers. The first product into
which they all divide exactly is the lowest common
denominator.

8. Modify the paint estimation example to input the lengths and heights of doors and windows in the room, calculate their areas and subtract them from the total before calculating the amount of paint. Also input the cost of a litre of paint, and calculate the total cost.

9. Write a program like the paint estimation one to estimate the number of rolls of wallpaper needed to paper a room, and the cost.

Section 5B
Interactive programs

A major advantage of terminals and microcomputers is that they can be used for programs where both the computer and the programmer take part in the solution of a problem. Programs of this type are called interactive programs.

Example 5B

Write a program to test your ability to guess the answer to a division sum (to the nearest whole number). The two numbers to be divided are first put in, followed by a series of guesses. If a guess is too high, the computer prints TOO HIGH and for guesses too low, it prints TOO LOW. If a guess is near enough, the correct answer is printed, and two new input numbers are supplied. The program stops if required to divide by zero.

Method

The condition "to the nearest whole number" means an error of less than 0·5. Thus a guess is rejected if it is less than the correct answer minus 0·5 or greater than the correct answer plus 0·5. This requires two condition statements.

Flow diagram

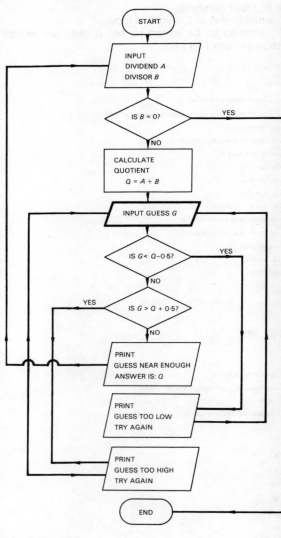

Variables

A: dividend B: divisor Q: quotient
G: guess of quotient

Program

```
 5    PRINT "TYPE IN TWO NUMBERS"
10    INPUT A,B
15    IF B = 0 THEN 80
20    LET Q = A/B
25    PRINT "GUESS THE ANSWER OF"; A; "/"; B
30    INPUT G
35    IF G<Q – 0.5 THEN 60
40    IF G>Q + 0.5 THEN 70
45    PRINT "NEAR ENOUGH , ANSWER IS"; Q
50    PRINT "TYPE IN TWO MORE NUMBERS, ZEROS IF YOUVE HAD ENOUGH"
55    GO TO 10
60    PRINT "TOO LOW, GUESS AGAIN"
65    GO TO 30
70    PRINT "TOO HIGH, GUESS AGAIN"
75    GO TO 30
80    STOP
85    END
```

Results

```
TYPE IN TWO NUMBERS
←85,13
GUESS THE ANSWER OF 85/13
←7
NEAR ENOUGH, ANSWER IS 6.53846
TYPE IN TWO MORE NUMBERS, ZEROS IF YOUVE HAD ENOUGH
←65,11
GUESS THE ANSWER OF 65/11
←5
TOO LOW, GUESS AGAIN
←7
TOO HIGH, GUESS AGAIN
←6
NEAR ENOUGH, ANSWER IS 5.90909
TYPE IN TWO MORE NUMBERS, ZEROS IF YOUVE HAD ENOUGH
←0,0
STOPPED AT LINE 80
```

Exercise 5B

1. Write a program to test your ability to guess the square root of a number. Choose a suitable error margin (say $0 \cdot 1$). If the guess is more than $\cdot 1$ above the actual root, the message TOO HIGH is printed, if more than $\cdot 1$ below the actual root, TOO LOW. Otherwise the correct root is printed with the message NEAR ENOUGH.

☐ 2. Write a program to find a solution of an equation by estimation. For example, if the equation is $3x^2 + 4x - 10 = 0$, input an estimated value of x, calculate $y = 3x^2 + 4x - 10$ and print y. From the value of y, decide on an improved estimate of x. Continue until the value of y is close enough to zero.

3. As Question 1, but testing your ability to guess the reciprocal of a number.

$$r = \frac{1}{x}$$

r: reciprocal x: number

☐ 4. When the accelerator of a car is pressed, its speed changes according to the equation:

$$d = a - \cdot 125v$$

d: change of speed in one second
a: accelerator setting (0 to 5) v: speed (m/s)

On braking, the same equation applies, with a negative value of a (0 to −5), thus making d negative and reducing the speed.

Starting with speed, distance and time all zero, input a series of values of a, simulating accelerating and braking the car at one second intervals. Work out the change of speed as above, and the current speed and distance travelled from the start, as follows:

speed: $w = v + d$
distance: $x = \frac{1}{2}(v + w)$
total distance: $u = s + x$
time: $t = t + 1$

w: new speed (m/s) v: old speed (m/s)
d: change of speed, from previous equation (m/s)
x: distance travelled during current second (m)
u: new total distance (m)
s: previous total distance (m) t: time (s)

Print t, w and u, then put $v = w$ and $s = u$, and input a new acceleration. The program stops when an accelerator setting out of range (less than −5 or more than 5) is input.

Use your program to find the top speed of the car, and the shortest time to reach top speed. Simulate driving at various constant speeds, and stopping in a certain distance.

Note: 1 m/s $\simeq$ 2 mph.

☐ 5. A sum of money saved with compound interest will increase by the formula:

$$A = P\left(1 + \frac{R}{100}\right)^t$$

A: amount (£) after t years P: initial amount (£)
R: interest rate (%) t: time (years)

(a) Input a sum of money and an interest rate, and by trying different values of the time, find how long it will take to double its initial amount.

(b) Input a sum of money and a time, and try different interest rates to see at what rate the sum will double its initial amount during that time.

6. (a) Each of the following lines of BASIC contains an error. Say what is wrong in each case.

   (i) 100 INPUT N; D
   (ii) 100 GO TO 100
   (iii) 100 PRINT JOHN
   (iv) 100 LET D+2=5
   (v) 100 LET A=(A+B) (A−B)

(b) The following program should read 50 numbers and print out a message saying how many of them are greater than 10. It contains four logical errors which prevent the program from working correctly. Write a correct version.

```
10  LET N=0
20  FOR X=1 TO 50
30  INPUT A(X)
40  NEXT X
50  FOR Y=1 TO 50
60  IF A(Y)>=10 THEN 80
70  GO TO 100
80  LET N=N+1
90  PRINT "THERE ARE"; N; "NUMBERS
                              >TEN"
100 NEXT Y
110 END
```

(East Anglian Examinations Board)

6. Lists

Lists of prices, bank balances, names and other information occur frequently in programs. It is inconvenient to refer to each item by a different letter, particularly as the lists are sometimes long. This chapter introduces a method of storing lists of information which makes it easy to use loops for calculations with entire lists, and also to refer to any single number in a list.

Flow diagram

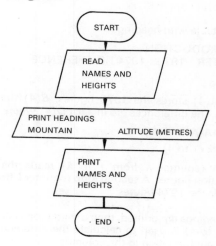

Section 6A
Dimensions

The statement

DIM A(3)

where DIM is short for dimension, creates a list of three variables: $A(1)$, $A(2)$ and $A(3)$. The statement

DIM L$(4)

creates a list of four variables, each of which stores words.

The DIM statement must be the first statement of a program.

Example 6A1

Store on a computer lists of the names and heights of four mountains. Print this information.

Method

A list M$(4) stores the names, a list $H(4)$ the heights (in metres).

Program

```
5 DIM M$(4),H(4)
10 READ M$(1),H(1),M$(2),H(2),M$(3),H(3),M$(4),H(4)
15 PRINT "MOUNTAIN","ALTITUDE (METRES)"
18 PRINT
20 PRINT M$(1),H(1)
25 PRINT M$(2),H(2)
30 PRINT M$(3),H(3)
35 PRINT M$(4),H(4)
40 STOP
45 DATA "MT EVEREST    ",9063
50 DATA "MT BLANC      ",4924
55 DATA "MT MITCHELL   ",2086
60 DATA "MT ACONCAGUA",7129
65 END
*
```

Results

```
MOUNTAIN        ALTITUDE (METRES)

MT EVEREST      9063
MT BLANC        4924
MT MITCHELL     2086
MT ACONCAGUA    7129
```

Points to notice
● One DIM statement declares both lists.

Index variables

A variable may be used to refer to a member of a list. For example $A(N)$ is $A(1)$ or $A(2)$ or $A(3)$ depending on the value of N. A variable used like N is called an *index* (or sometimes a *pointer*). It is frequently a loop counter, and allows lists to be used in loops.

Example 6A2

A data card contains the number of cars produced at a factory during the four quarters of 1975. Another card contains the corresponding figures for 1974.

Write a program to read this information into suitable lists, and calculate the difference between the 1975 figures for each quarter and the corresponding 1974 figure.

Print a table with headings

CAR PRODUCTION
QUARTER 1975 1974 DIFFERENCE

Method

A list $A(4)$ stores the 1975 figures, $B(4)$ the 1974 figures. The differences are in a list $D(4)$ where

$D(N) = A(N) - B(N)$

N: index (1 to 4)

A loop (counter K from 1 to 4) reads the 1975 production figures. A second loop (counter L from 1 to 4) reads the 1974 figures.

The headings are printed, then a third loop (counter N from 1 to 4) is used to calculate the differences and print the information in the columns.

Flow diagram

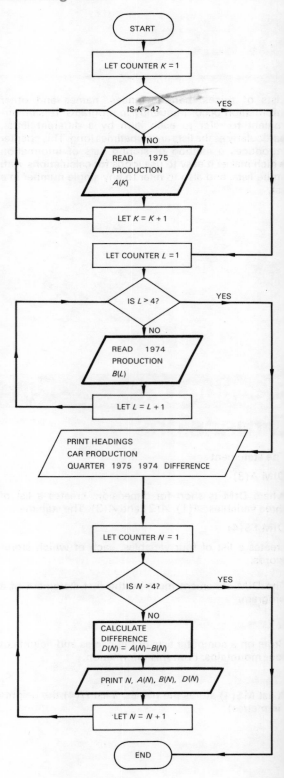

Variables

K: counter and index (1 to 4)
A(4): 1975 production
L: counter and index (1 to 4)
B(4): 1974 production
N: counter and index (1 to 4)
D(4): difference in production

Program

```
5 DIM A(4),B(4),D(4)
10 FOR K=1 TO 4 STEP 1
15 READ A(K)
20 NEXT K
25 FOR L=1 TO 4 STEP 1
30 READ B(L)
35 NEXT L
40 PRINT "CAR PRODUCTION"
45 PRINT
50 PRINT "QUARTER","1975","1974","DIFFERENCE"
55 PRINT
60 FOR N=1 TO 4 STEP 1
65 LET D(N)=A(N)-B(N)
70 PRINT N,A(N),B(N),D(N)
75 NEXT N
80 STOP
85 DATA 8762,9117,7162,8473
90 DATA 7991,8032,7275,7943
95 END
*
```

Results

```
CAR PRODUCTION

QUARTER     1975        1974        DIFFERENCE

1           8762        7991        771
2           9117        8032        1085
3           7162        7275        -113
4           8473        7943        530
```

Repeated calculations

An important use of lists is for storing numbers which are used in more than one calculation. This avoids the need for RESTORE statements and reading the numbers a second or third time.

Example 6A3

Read a set of 16 numbers and calculate by what percentage each number differs from the average. Print a list of the numbers and the percentage differences.

Method

A list A(16) stores the numbers, P(16) the percentages. A loop is used to read the numbers, another to add up the total, after which the average is calculated. In a third loop, the percentage differences are calculated by the formula:

$$P(N) = \frac{(A(N) - M) \times 100}{M}$$

N: index (1 to 16)
P(N): percentage difference
A(N): number   M: average

In a fourth loop, the numbers and percentages are printed.

Variables

K, L, N, R: counters and index numbers
A(16): numbers   P(16): percentages
T: total   M: average

Flow diagram

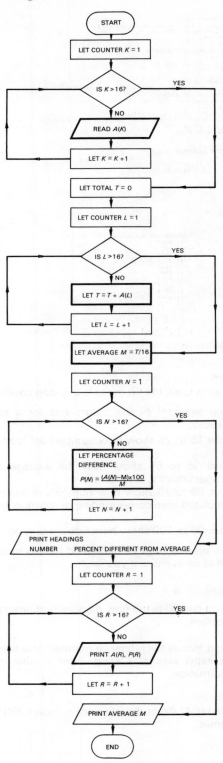

Program

```
5 DIM A(16),P(16)
10 REM FIRST LOOP READS IN VALUES OF A
15 FOR K=1 TO 16 STEP 1
20 READ A(K)
25 NEXT K
30 REM SECOND LOOP ADDS UP TOTAL
35 LET T=0
40 FOR L=1 TO 16 STEP 1
45 LET T=T+A(L)
50 NEXT L
55 LET M=T/16
60 REM THIRD LOOP CALULATES PERCENTAGE DIFFERENCES
65 FOR N=1 TO 16 STEP 1
70 LET P(N)=(A(N)-M)/M*100
75 NEXT N
80 REM FOURTH LOOP PRINTS RESULTS
85 PRINT "NUMBER","PERCENTAGE DIFFERENT FROM AVERAGE"
90 FOR R=1 TO 16 STEP 1
95 PRINT A(R),P(R)
100 NEXT R
105 PRINT
110 PRINT "AVERAGE : ";M
115 STOP
120 DATA 5,11,7,2,3,15,10,23
125 DATA 17,9,18,2,41,20,16,11
130 END
```

Results

```
NUMBER          PERCENTAGE DIFFERENT FROM AVERAGE
5                   -61.9048
11                  -16.1905
7                   -46.6667
2                   -84.7619
3                   -77.1429
15                   14.2857
10                  -23.8095
23                   75.2381
17                   29.5238
9                   -31.4286
18                   37.1429
2                   -84.7619
41                  212.381
20                   52.381
16                   21.9048
11                  -16.1905

AVERAGE :  13.125
```

Points to notice

● In each loop, the list index is the loop counter.

● Each segment of the program is for a specific purpose:

Lines 15 to 25 show how numbers are read into a list

Lines 35 to 55 show how the average of the numbers in a list is worked out

Lines 65 to 75 show how numbers in one list are calculated from corresponding numbers in another list

Lines 90 to 100 show how lists are printed.

● This program can be shortened to two loops. Do this as an exercise if you wish.

Exercise 6A

Copy and complete the flow diagram and program for this problem:

1. Read lists of the reference numbers and names of six items kept at a shop. Print a table of this information.

Method

A list $R(6)$ stores the reference numbers, N$(6) the names.

A loop is used to read the information, another to print it.

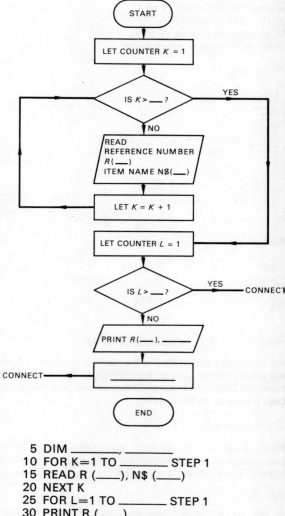

```
 5 DIM _____, _____
10 FOR K=1 TO _____ STEP 1
15 READ R (___), N$ (___)
20 NEXT K
25 FOR L=1 TO _____ STEP 1
30 PRINT R (___), _____
35 _____
40 STOP
45 DATA 4167, "POWER DRILL"
50 DATA 5215, "SAW"
55 DATA ____, "HAMMER"
60 _____
65 _____
70 _____
75 END
```

Study these programs carefully and write down the numbers in each list at the end of each program.

2.
```
 5 DIM B(4), C(4), D(4)
10 FOR K=1 TO 4 STEP 1
15 READ B(K)
20 NEXT K
25 FOR N=1 TO 4 STEP 1
30 READ C(N)
35 LET D(N)=B(N)+C(N)
40 NEXT N
45 FOR R=1 TO 4 STEP 1
50 PRINT D(R)
55 NEXT R
60 STOP
65 DATA 7, 4, 9, 15
70 DATA 3, 8, 11, 1
75 END
```

3.
```
 5 DIM X(5), Y(5)
10 FOR K=1 TO 5 STEP 1
15 LET X(K)=K+1
20 LET Y(K)=3*K
25 PRINT X(K), Y(K)
30 NEXT K
35 STOP
40 END
```

4.
```
  5 DIM A(4), T(4)
 10 FOR K=1 TO 4 STEP 1
 15 LET T(K)=0
 20 NEXT K
 25 FOR L=1 TO 3 STEP 1
 30 FOR M=1 TO 4 STEP 1
 35 READ A(M)
 40 PRINT A(M),
 45 LET T(M)=T(M)+A(M)
 50 NEXT M
 55 PRINT
 60 NEXT L
 65 FOR N=1 TO 4 STEP 1
 70 PRINT T(N),
 75 NEXT N
 80 STOP
 85 DATA 8, 14, 36, 2
 90 DATA 9, 11, 13, 17
 95 DATA 7, 4, 8, 3
100 END
```

5. Which of these variables are correct, and which will give errors?

$A(7)$, $B(M)$, $A\$(-2)$, $K(4)\$$, $X4$, $\$A(5)$, $K1(3)$, $A(X1)$, $PR(5)$, $H(A\$)$

Draw flow diagrams and write programs for some of these problems.

6. Find out the prices of four types of car. Write a program to read this information from data cards (one card has the name of a car and its price) into the lists N\$(4) for the names and $P(4)$ for the prices. Print a table of the information.

7. The numbers of people killed, seriously injured and slightly injured in road accidents in Britain during 1974 were 6876, 82030 and 235696. The corresponding figures for 1964 were 7820, 95460 and 282219.

Write a program to read the 1974 figures into the list $X(3)$ and the 1964 figures into the list $Y(3)$. Calculate the differences in the list $Z(3)$ where

$Z(N)=Y(N)-X(N)$

N: index (1 to 3)

Print a table with headings

ROAD ACCIDENTS IN BRITAIN
NUMBERS KILLED
SERIOUSLY INJURED   SLIGHTLY INJURED
1974   1964   DIFFERENCE

8. The numbers in stock of small, medium, large and extra large size of a certain shirt at a clothes shop are read into the list $N(4)$, and the price of each size into the list $P(4)$. The stock value of each size is stored in the list $V(4)$, where:

$V(K)=N(K)\times P(K)$

K: index from 1 to 4

The total stock value is added up, and a table printed with headings: (size 1 is small, 2 medium, etc.)

SIZE	NO. IN STOCK	PRICE	STOCK	VALUE
..	..		..	..	..
.					
.					

TOTAL STOCK VALUE: ..

The list A\$(4) can be used to store the size names (A\$(1)="SMALL" etc.).

9. The heights of ten trees are measured after one year, two years and three years, and read into the lists $A(10)$, $B(10)$, $C(10)$ respectively. The amounts of growth during the second and third years, $G(10)$ and $H(10)$ are calculated from

$G(N)=B(N)-A(N)$
$H(N)=C(N)-B(N)$

N: index from 1 to 10

A table is printed with headings:

TREE NO.   HEIGHT 1   HEIGHT 2   HEIGHT 3
                               GROWTH 2   GROWTH 3

Modification

Calculate the averages of the heights and growths.

10. A survey is carried out to find the average family size of the pupils in a class. A list $F(6)$ is read, where $F(1)$ is the number of pupils with families of 1 child, $F(2)$ the number with families of two children, etc. This information is printed under the headings:

FAMILY SIZE   NUMBER OF FAMILIES

The average family size is calculated as follows:

The total number of families:
$$T1 = F(1) + F(2) + \ldots + F(6)$$

The total number of children in all the families:
$$T2 = 1 \times F(1) + 2 \times F(2) + \ldots + 6 \times F(6)$$

The average family size:

$$A = \frac{T2}{T1}$$

The two totals and the average are printed.

11. Three branches of a newsagent each sell six daily newspapers. For each branch, a data card is prepared with its weekly sales of the six papers. The lists $A(6)$, $B(6)$, $C(6)$ record this information ($A(3)$ is the sales of branch A of newspaper 3). The combined sales for each newspaper from the three branches are calculated and stored in the list $T(6)$:

$$T(N) = A(N) + B(N) + C(N)$$

N: index from 1 to 6

The information is printed under the headings

PAPER NUMBER   BRANCH A   BRANCH B   BRANCH C   TOTAL

Suggestions for further programs

Programs from Exercise 2E (page 25) may be re-written using lists to store the data, eliminating RESTORE statements and the necessity of reading the data a second or third time.

Section 6B
Further problems using lists

The problems in this section give some idea how computers are used in practice to handle large quantities of information (known as data processing). This information would normally be stored on a magnetic tape or magnetic disc. It will be seen that the actual calculations form a relatively small part of the program and are often nothing more than simple additions. Most of the program is concerned with finding the right information at the right time, putting the results in the right place, and making the output easy to read.

Checks are often put into the program, so that wrong input data is simply ignored, rather than stopping the whole program.

Example 6B1

The balances of 20 bank accounts are stored in a list, in order of account number from 1 to 20. Write a program to read this list, and then read a series of deposits or withdrawals, each with an account number and an amount (positive for deposit, negative for withdrawal). For each transaction, the account number, amount deposited or withdrawn and new balance are printed. The transactions end when the account number -1 is read. A list of new balances is then printed.

Method
The list $B(20)$ stores the 20 balances.

Using the variable A (account number) as a loop counter from 1 to 20, values of $B(A)$ are read and printed as a check.

A series of values of account number N and transaction T (deposit or withdrawal) are read. If the account number is over 20, the transaction is ignored. Since withdrawals are negative numbers, T is added to $B(N)$ to give the new balance.

A loop using account number C as counter prints the new balances $B(C)$.

Flow diagram

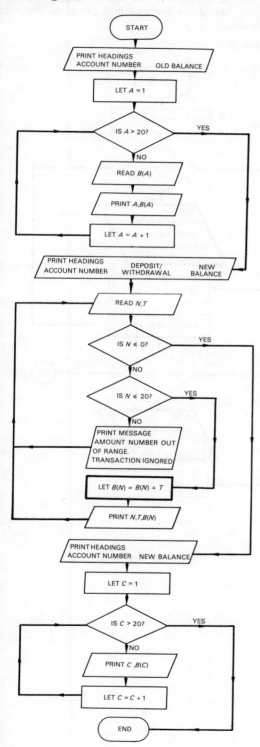

Variables

$B(20)$: balances (£)
A: counter (account number)
N: account number
T: deposit or withdrawal (£)
C: counter (account number)

Program

```
2 PAGE
5 DIM B(20)
10 PRINT "ACCOUNT NUMBER","OLD BALANCE"
15 FOR A=1 TO 20 STEP 1
20 READ B(A)
25 PRINT A,B(A)
30 NEXT A
35 PRINT
40 PRINT
45 PRINT "ACCOUNT NUMBER","DEPOSIT/WITHDRAWAL","NEW BALANCE"
50 READ N,T
55 IF N<=0 THEN 90
60 IF N<=20 THEN 75
65 PRINT "ACCOUNT NUMBER OUT OF RANGE...TRANSACTION IGNORED"
70 GO TO 50
75 LET B(N)=B(N)+T
80 PRINT N,T,,B(N)
85 GO TO 50
90 PRINT
95 PRINT
100 PRINT "ACCOUNT NUMBER","NEW BALANCE"
105 FOR C=1 TO 20 STEP 1
110 PRINT C,B(C)
115 NEXT C
120 STOP
125 DATA 365.12,47.38,95.00,117.25,5612.00,47.22,962.17,63.15,12.09,311.11
130 DATA 153.61,296.00,21.36,19.51,793.25,9662.00,31.32,83.17,150.26,13.20
135 DATA 5,-21.26
140 DATA 7,116.75
145 DATA 2,-11.67
150 DATA 17,33.91
155 DATA 11,-31.24
160 DATA 31,25.15
165 DATA 7,-31.62
170 DATA 15,361.14
175 DATA -1,0
180 END
*
```

Results

```
ACCOUNT NUMBER OLD BALANCE
1              365.12
2              47.38
3              95
4              117.25
5              5612
6              47.22
7              962.17
8              63.15
9              12.09
10             311.11
11             153.61
12             296
13             21.36
14             19.51
15             793.25
16             9662
17             31.32
18             83.17
19             150.26
20             13.2


ACCOUNT NUMBER DEPOSIT/WITHDRAWAL        NEW BALANCE
5              -21.26                    5590.74
7              116.75                    1078.92
2              -11.67                    35.71
17             33.91                     65.23
11             -31.24                    122.37
ACCOUNT NUMBER OUT OF RANGE...TRANSACTION IGNORED
7              -31.62                    1047.3
15             361.14                    1154.39


ACCOUNT NUMBER NEW BALANCE
1              365.12
2              35.71
3              95
4              117.25
5              5590.74
6              47.22
7              1047.3
8              63.15
9              12.09
10             311.11
11             122.37
12             296
13             21.36
14             19.51
15             1154.39
16             9662
17             65.23
18             83.17
19             150.26
20             13.2
```

Points to notice

● The list of balances is used three times in the program. In two cases (statements 15 to 30 and 105 to 115) the list is used in order, the index being a loop counter. In the other (statements 50 to 75) the numbers on the list are not used in order. They are referred to by an index that is part of the input data. The first two cases are of *serial access* of stored data, the third of *random access*.

● Statement 60 safeguards against wrong account numbers (greater than 20), ignoring the transaction they describe, and printing a message to notify the programmer of the error.

● The first two data statements contain the 20 old balances, in order of account number. The subsequent data statements deal with one transaction each.

● The two commas in print statement 80 cause a column to be skipped, since the heading DEPOSIT/WITHDRAWAL is wider than one column.

Example 6B2

Each of the ten workers at a factory has a record card with his or her works number (between 1 and 10), name, ordinary rate per hour and overtime rate per hour.

At the end of every week, a card is prepared for each worker with his or her works number, number of ordinary hours worked and number of overtime hours worked.

Write a program to read the ten rates cards, then the ten hours cards, and calculate the ordinary pay, overtime pay and total pay for each worker. Neither set of data cards is in order of works number.

Method

Lists are used to store:

N$(10): name   R(10): ordinary rate
V(10): overtime rate   H(10): ordinary hours
J(10): overtime hours

The works number W is the index for all lists.

Lists are not used for the pay, as it is printed as soon as it is calculated.

ordinary pay: $P = R(W) \times H(W)$
overtime pay: $M = V(W) \times J(W)$
total pay: $T = P + M$

The stages of the program are:

● A loop (counter $K1$ from 1 to 10) reads the works numbers, names and pay rates.

● A loop (counter $K2$ from 1 to 10) reads the works numbers and hours.

● A loop (counter W, the works number, from 1 to 10) calculates the pay and prints all the information.

Flow diagram

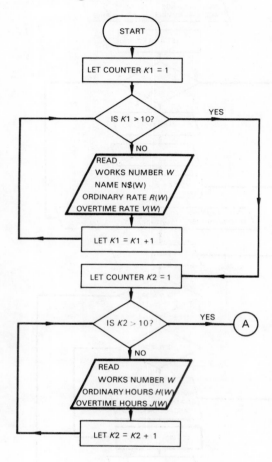

Flowchart

(A)

PRINT HEADINGS

WORKS NO.　NAME　ORD. RATE　OVER. RATE　ORD. HRS.　OVER. HRS.　PAY (£)

LET COUNTER
(WORKS NUMBER)
$W = 1$

IS $W > 10$? —YES→

NO

CALCULATE
ORDINARY PAY
$P = R(W) \times H(W)$

CALCULATE
OVERTIME PAY
$M = V(W) \times J(W)$

CALCULATE
TOTAL PAY
$T = P + M$

PRINT
W, N$(W), $R(W)$, $V(W)$, $H(W)$, $J(W)$, T

LET $W = W + 1$

END

Program

```
2 PAGE
5 DIM N$(10),R(10),V(10),H(10),J(10)
10 FOR K1=1 TO 10 STEP 1
15 READ W,N$(W),R(W),V(W)
20 NEXT K1
25 FOR K2=1 TO 10 STEP 1
30 READ W,H(W),J(W)
35 NEXT K2
40 PRINT "WORKS NO.","NAME","ORD. RATE","OVER. RATE",
45 PRINT "ORD.HRS.","OVER. HRS.","PAY (£)"
50 PRINT
55 FOR W=1 TO 10 STEP 1
60 LET P=R(W)*H(W)
65 LET M=V(W)*J(W)
70 LET T=P+M
75 PRINT W,N$(W),R(W),V(W),H(W),J(W),T
80 NEXT W
85 STOP
101 DATA  7,"A.FRAMPTON   ",1.27,1.92
102 DATA  3,"L.MILLS      ",1.49,2.23
103 DATA  4,"J.HARTLEY    ",1.14,1.75
104 DATA  1,"K.WEBBER     ",2.42,3.72
105 DATA  9,"M.EDKINS     ",1.63,2.57
106 DATA  2,"S.KENT       ",1.18,1.70
107 DATA  5,"E.KENNEDY    ",2.02,3.13
108 DATA  8,"P.MACKAY     ",0.96,1.42
109 DATA  6,"T.REID       ",1.33,2.04
110 DATA 10,"R.STEVENSON  ",1.47,2.26
111 DATA  4,38.75, 0.00
112 DATA  6,40.00, 4.50
113 DATA  1,37.25, 0.00
114 DATA  5,40.00,11.75
115 DATA  9,27.50, 0.00
116 DATA 10,40.00, 1.25
117 DATA  3,40.00, 3.00
118 DATA  8,40.00, 4.75
119 DATA  2,33.75, 0.00
120 DATA  7,40.00,12.50
200 END
*
```

Points to notice

● The first ten data cards will not change much from week to week. This is called *master data*.

● The program combines information from the first ten cards with information from the second ten.

Results

WORKS NO.	NAME	ORD. RATE	OVER. RATE	ORD.HRS.	OVER. HRS.	PAY (£)
1	K.WEBBER	2.42	3.72	37.25	0	90.145
2	S.KENT	1.18	1.7	33.75	0	39.825
3	L.MILLS	1.49	2.23	40	3	66.29
4	J.HARTLEY	1.14	1.75	38.75	0	44.175
5	E.KENNEDY	2.02	3.13	40	11.75	117.577
6	T.REID	1.33	2.04	40	4.5	62.38
7	A.FRAMPTON	1.27	1.92	40	12.5	74.8
8	P.MACKAY	.96	1.42	40	4.75	45.145
9	M.EDKINS	1.63	2.57	27.5	0	44.825
10	R.STEVENSON	1.47	2.26	40	1.25	61.625

Exercise 6B

Copy and complete the flow diagram and program for this problem.

1. At a paint factory, the seven colours produced are mixed from different ratios of four dyes. The fractions of each dye for a colour are recorded on a data card, together with its colour code (from 1 to 7). For example

   DATA 3, ·37, ·18, ·09, ·36

   gives the mixture for colour number 3. The fractions must add up to 1.

   Orders for paint contain an order number, colour code and quantity (litres). For example

   DATA 4316, 4, 750

   is an order for 750 litres of colour number 4.

   Write a program to read the seven ratio cards, and then a number of order cards (end marked by order number 0). For each order, calculate the number of litres of each dye required. Print a table of:

   ORDER NO.   COLOUR CODE   DYE 1   DYE 2
   DYE 3   DYE 4

Variables

R: colour code and list index
$A(7)$: fraction of dye 1 in the seven colours
$B(7)$: fraction of dye 2 in the seven colours
$C(7)$: fraction of dye 3 in the seven colours
$D(7)$: fraction of dye 4 in the seven colours
N: order number Q: quantity ordered
$L1$: number of litres of dye 1
$L2$: number of litres of dye 2
$L3$: number of litres of dye 3
$L4$: number of litres of dye 4
K: loop counter

Formulae

$L1 = Q \times A(R)$
$L2 = Q \times B(R)$
$L3 = Q \times C(R)$
$L4 = Q \times D(R)$

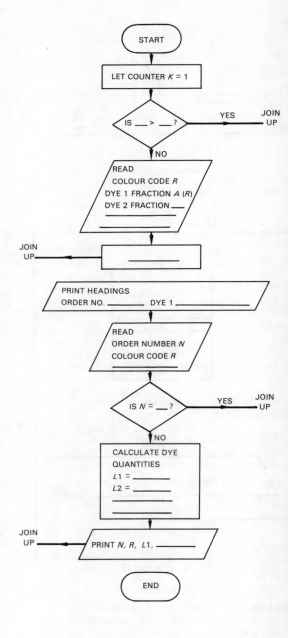

```
 5 DIM A(7), _____
10 FOR K=1 TO _____ STEP _____
15 READ R, A(R), B(R), _____
20 NEXT _____
25 PRINT "ORDER NO.", "_____",
              "DYE 1", _____
30 READ N, R, _____
35 IF N=_____ THEN _____
40 LET L1=_____
45 LET L2=_____
   _____
   _____
60 PRINT N, R, L1, _____
65 GO TO _____
70 STOP
75 DATA 3, ·37, ·18, ·09, ·36
80 DATA _____
85 DATA _____
90 DATA _____
95 DATA _____
100 DATA _____
105 DATA 2, ·68, ·02, ·13, ·17
110 DATA 4316, 4, 750
115 DATA _____
    _____
    _____
    _____
```

Draw flow diagrams and write programs for some of these problems.

2. A company has nine telephone extensions. Store a list of the offices and people reached by the extensions, read from data cards. For example

DATA 5, "CHIEF ACCOUNTANT", "MR. A. M.
                          BROWN"

gives the office and name of the person on extension 5.

Then read an extension number and print the office and name of the person on that extension.

Variables

E: extension number and list index
$F\$(9)$: offices on the nine extensions
$N\$(9)$: names of people on the nine extensions
$K(1$ to $9)$: loop counter

3. At a shop, the prices of 20 items are stored on a data card (or cards) in order of item number. For each sale, a sale data card is prepared with an item number and quantity sold. Write a program to read the price card, followed by a number of sale cards, and calculate the cost (cost=price × quantity) for each sale. Print a table with headings

ITEM NUMBER   PRICE   QUANTITY   COST

4. Salesmen at a firm are paid commission as follows:

8% of the first £1000 of their monthly sales
20% of the rest

Read a list of the names of six salesmen, in order of salesman number, from 1 to 6. Use the list N$(6) and put each name in inverted commas in the data statements. Then read six sales cards, each with a salesman number and four weekly sales figures. The sales cards are not in order of salesman number.

Calculate the month's total sales, and commission due to each salesman. Print a list of the information for each salesman, set out as follows:

SALESMAN NUMBER: ...
NAME: ...
WEEKLY SALES FIGURES: ... ...
TOTAL SALES: ...   COMMISSION: ...

☐ **5.** A record is kept of the production of each of the eight machines at a factory. At the end of a week, a data card is prepared for each machine, with machine number (from 1 to 8), number of items produced and number of running hours. These cards are read, not necessarily in order of machine number. The number of items is stored in the list $P(8)$, and the hours in the list $H(8)$.

● Calculate the number of items per hour for each machine (use the list $R(8)$).

● Add up the total production and total hours worked.

● Calculate the average production per hour.

average production=total production÷total hours

● Print a list, in order of machine number, of

MACHINE NUMBER	PRODUCTION	HOURS	PRODUCTION/ HOUR
1	...	...	...
2	...	...	...
.			
.			
.			
TOTAL	...	...	...

Section 6C
Counting frequencies for histograms

Histograms are often used to show the number of times (the frequency) that a certain quantity occurs. These frequencies are conveniently counted using lists.

Example 6C1

The number of children in the family of each pupil in a class is recorded. Write a program to read these numbers (end marked -1), count the number of families with 1 child, 2 children, . . . up to 7 children, and print a table and a histogram of the results.

Method

A list $N(7)$ stores the numbers of each family size: $N(1)$ is the number of families with 1 child, etc.

Each part of the program forms a separate segment.

Segment 1

The numbers of each family size are first set to zero. Each family size is then read, and the appropriate number increased by 1. Family sizes greater than seven are ignored.

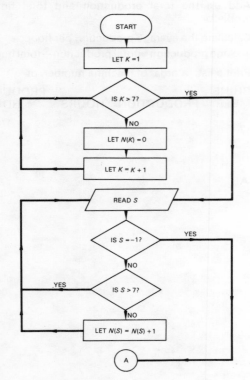

Variables

K: counter (1 to 7)
$N(K)$: number of families of size K
S: size of a family

Note: The last symbol on the flow diagram is connector, showing that the diagram is continue elsewhere.

Segment 2

A loop is used to print the number of families of eac size, with suitable headings.

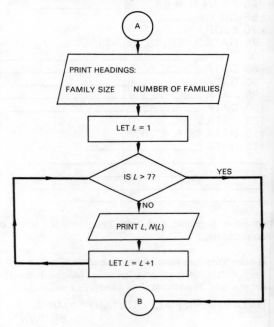

Variables

L: loop counter (1 to 7)
$N(L)$: number of families of size L

Segment 3

A loop of variable length is used to print a row of *'s for each family size, one * for each family of that size. The length of loop 1 is $N(1)$. An outer loop counts through the family sizes.

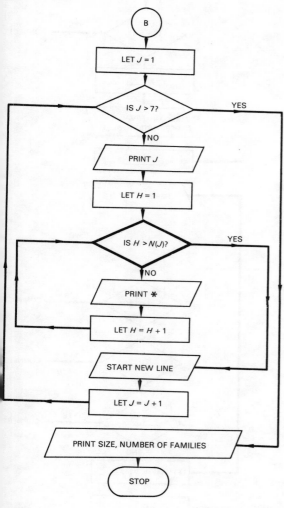

Variables

J: counter (family size, 1 to 7)
H: counter (number of families of size J)

Program

```
2 PAGE
5 DIM N(7)
10 REM *** SEGMENT 1 ***
15 FOR K=1 TO 7 STEP 1
20 LET N(K)=0
25 NEXT K
30 READ S
35 IF S=-1 THEN 55
40 IF S>7 THEN 30
45 LET N(S)=N(S)+1
50 GO TO 30
55 REM *** SEGMENT 2 ***
60 PRINT "FAMILY SIZE","NUMBER IN CLASS"
65 FOR L=1 TO 7 STEP 1
70 PRINT L,N(L)
75 NEXT L
80 PRINT
85 PRINT
90 REM *** SEGMENT 3 ***
95 FOR J=1 TO 7 STEP 1
100 PRINT J,
110 FOR H=1 TO N(J) STEP 1
115 PRINT "*  ";
120 NEXT H
125 PRINT
130 PRINT
135 NEXT J
140 PRINT "FAMILY SIZE","NUMBER IN CLASS"
145 STOP
150 DATA 1,4,3,2,2,5,2,3,2,1
155 DATA 3,2,2,1,6,2,3,7,1,2
160 DATA 4,3,1,3,2,2,1,5,2,1
165 DATA 6,1,2,2,1,-1
170 END
*
```

Results

```
FAMILY SIZE     NUMBER IN CLASS
1                9
2                13
3                6
4                3
5                2
6                1
7                1


1               *  *  *  *  *  *  *  *  *
2               *  *  *  *  *  *  *  *  *  *  *  *  *
3               *  *  *  *  *  *
4               *  *  *
5               *  *
6               *
7               *
FAMILY SIZE     NUMBER IN CLASS
```

Points to notice

● The histogram is spaced out by the two blank spaces inside the inverted commas in line 115. Thus there is a star every three spaces across the page.

● Spacing down the page is achieved by the blank PRINT statements 125 and 130.

● This program can be extended to calculate the percentage of each family size of the total, and the average family size.

Exercise 6C

Copy and complete the flow diagram and program for this problem:

1. Read a set of heights (centimetres) of the members of your class, and count the number in each of these intervals:

   less than 130 cm
   130 cm to 145 cm
   146 cm to 160 cm
   more than 160 cm

97

Print a histogram of the number of pupils in each height interval. The end of the list is marked by the height 0.

Method

The list $N(4)$ stores the numbers in the four height intervals. A list $I\$(4)$ stores the description of the intervals.

A loop is used to read the descriptions and set the numbers in each interval to zero.

A height (variable H) is read and tested to see if it is the end of the list. Three conditions decide which number is increased by 1:

Is $H < 130$? If so, increase $N(1)$ by 1
If not: Is $H < 146$? If so, increase $N(2)$ by 1
If not: Is $H < 161$? If so, increase $N(3)$ by 1
If not, increase $N(4)$ by 1.

The next height is then read.

Nested loops, the inner one of variable length, are used to print the histogram, as in the example

```
  5 DIM N(_____), I(_____)
 10 FOR K=1 TO 4 STEP 1
 15 LET N(_____)=_____
 20 READ I$(____)
 25 NEXT ____
 30 READ H
 35 IF H=_____ THEN _____
 40 IF H<130 THEN _____
 45 IF H_____ THEN _____
 50 IF _____
 55 LET N(4)=N(4)+_____
 60 GO TO 30
 65 LET N(__)=N(__)+_____
 70 GO TO _____
 75 LET _____
 80 GO TO ____
 85 LET _____
 90 _____
 95 PRINT "HEIGHT INTERVAL", "NUMBER
                             IN CLASS"
100 FOR L=1 TO ____ STEP 1
105 PRINT I$(—),
110 FOR M=1 TO N(__) STEP 1
115 PRINT "*" _____
120 NEXT _____
125 PRINT
130 _____
135 STOP
140 DATA "LESS THAN 130 CM"
145 DATA "_____"
150 DATA "_____"
155 DATA "_____"
160 DATA _____
165 DATA _____
170 END
```

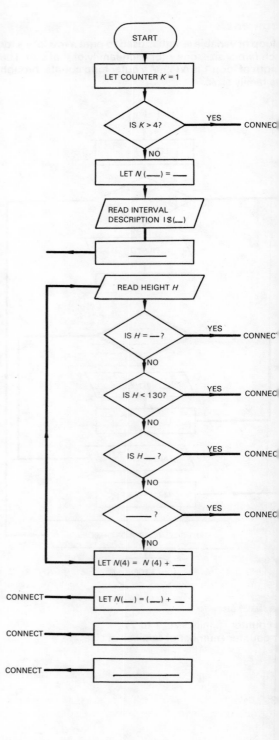

START

LET COUNTER $K = 1$

IS $K > 4$? — YES → CONNEC

NO

LET $N(\_\_) = \_\_$

READ INTERVAL DESCRIPTION I$(__)

_____

READ HEIGHT H

IS $H = \_\_$? — YES → CONNEC

NO

IS $H < 130$? — YES → CONNEC

NO

IS $H \_\_$? — YES → CONNEC

NO

____ ? — YES → CONNEC

NO

LET $N(4) = N(4) + \_\_$

CONNECT — LET $N(\_\_) = (\_\_) + \_\_$

CONNECT — _____

CONNECT — _____

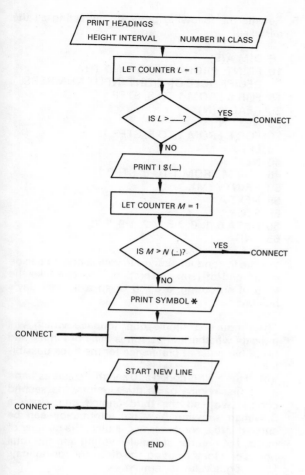

Draw flow diagrams and write programs for some of these problems:

2. Make a survey of the number of occupants in the cars passing in a road over a period of time. Read a list of these numbers (end marked 0) and count the number of cars with 1 occupant, the number with 2 occupants . . . up to 8 occupants. Print a histogram of the results.

Modification

Calculate the percentage of the total with 1 occupant, etc. and the average number of occupants. Print a histogram of the percentages.

3. Make a survey of the ages of the cars on a road by recording the last letter of their registration numbers and using this to determine their age. Read the ages (end marked −1) and count the numbers in the groups:

less than 2 years old
2 to 5 years old
6 to 10 years old
more than 10 years old.

Print a histogram of these results.

Modification

Write part of the program to convert the registration letters to the ages.

4. Other ideas for histograms are:
- distances of homes from school
- months of birthdays
- amounts of pocket money
- favourite colours
- countries visited on holiday
- types of house heating
- favourite school subject
- political party supported
- football team supported
- use of local agricultural land

In all cases the programs are similar to the example or the first question in this exercise.

☐ 5. Write a general histogram program which can be used for a variety of purposes. All information and headings must be read from data.

Exercise 6D
General List Programs

1. A flour mill supplies ten different types of flour. Monthly records are kept of the sales of each type, as follows:

At the beginning of each month, the totals for each type (stored in the list $T(10)$) are set to zero. For each sale, the type number (between 1 and 10) and number of bags sold are printed on a data card. These are read, and the appropriate total increased by the number of bags sold. The end of the list is marked by the type number O.

Write a program to carry out this operation, and print the monthly totals at the end. Reject any data with a type number greater than ten.

Modification

Calculate the percentage of each type of the overall total.

2. A survey is conducted to see which of five types of car people prefer. The results are coded as follows:

1: Leyland   4: General Motors
2: Ford   5: Fiat
3: Datsun   6: Other

Obtain (or invent ...) a set of suitable results, terminating with the number zero.

Write a program to set a list of six totals each to zero, then read the results, increasing the appropriate total by 1. (If the result is read as the variable K, then $T(K)$ is increased by 1.) Print the final totals, with suitable headings.

Modifications

● Express each total as a percentage of the overall total, using a list $P(6)$ where

$$P(K) = \frac{T(K) \times 100}{G}$$

P: percentage T: total G: overall total

● Reject any input numbers greater than 6 or less than zero.

3. *Top of the pops*: Make up a list of ten record titles. Your top of the pops program first reads these titles into the list R$(10) where R$(1) is the title of record 1, etc.

Get a number of people to vote for their favourite title. Read these votes into the program as a series of numbers, ending with 0.

Set a count for each record to zero (use the list $T(10)$), and use it to count the number of votes for each record.

After reading the votes, use the method of Section 3F in Chapter 3 to find the record with the most votes:

Print: TOP OF THE POPS IS:

    ... ...

☐4. Write a short essay comparing the two methods of handling lists of numbers that have been introduced (Sections 2E and 7A), with regard to:

length of the program
amount of computer memory space required
running time of the program

Say under what circumstances you would use each method in preference to the other.

5. Rewrite the following program, correcting all the mistakes:

```
 5 DIM A(5)
10 PRINT: PROGRAM TO FIND THE
   RECIPROCLE OF EIGHT INPUT NUMBERS.
15 FOR K FROM 1 TO 8, STEP 1
20 READ A(N)
25 NEXT N
30 FOR L FROM 1 TO 8, STEP 1
35 LET A=1/A
40 NEXT A
45 FOR M FROM 1 TO 8, STEP 1
50 PRINT A(M),
55 NEXT A
55 STOP.
60 DATA 6, 1, 0, 7·5, 7·2, 1·9, 3·72.
65 END
```

6. You are to conduct a survey in your school to decide on an end-of-term celebration. This can take the form of an outing, a disco or an extra half-day's holiday.

(i) Produce a simple questionnaire which will indicate whether the person is male or female and his or her order of preference for the three possibilities.
(ii) If the male is coded as 0 and the female as 1 and if the first choice gains three points, the second choice two and the third choice one, draw a flowchart showing how the information can be entered into a computer to calculate the number of males, the number of females voting and the total points cast for the outing, the disco and the holiday. Use a rogue value to terminate.
(iii) If the greatest number of points was gained by the first choice, i.e. the outing, write a program in CESIL or BASIC to decide on the type of outing. The choice this time is the zoo, the seaside, or the theatre, but pupils may vote for one only. Your program should output the number of girls voting for each of the three options and the number of boys voting for them.

(East Anglian Examinations Board)

7. Information retrieval

One of the commonest uses of computers is to store information and retrieve various items on request. Although BASIC language is not the most suitable one for this purpose, it can be used, and this chapter gives some idea how information retrieval programs are written. The programs are generally simple, containing virtually no calculations.

The information, such as names and addresses, containing letters or numbers or both, is put in data statements, usually in inverted commas. It is read into variables such as A$ or B$(10). Sorting of information is usually done by condition statements.

The exercises in this chapter can be done in groups, with some pupils compiling the information and others writing the program. Pupils are encouraged to make up their own programs, using information relevant to them.

Several of the examples use the same set of information, and give an idea how a simple school records system might work.

Section 7A
Selecting information

Example 7A1

The following information is recorded for a group of 20 fourth year pupils:

NAME   SEX   DATE OF BIRTH   FORM

A typical set of data would be:

101 DATA "DAVID BROWN", "M", "14/3/62", "4B"

The forms are 4A, 4B and 4C.

Read these data, and print the name, sex and date of birth of all the pupils in form 4A.

Method

A loop is used to read the data, and print the required information if the form is 4A.

Flow diagram

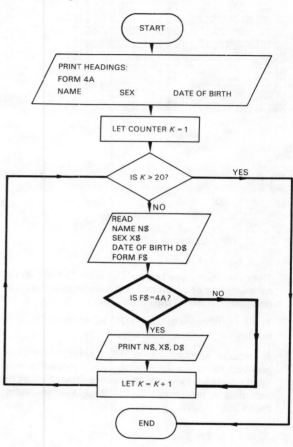

Variables

K: counter   N$: name   X$: sex
D$: date of birth   F$: form

Program

```
5 PRINT "FORM 4A"
10 PRINT
15 PRINT "NAME","SEX","DATE OF BIRTH"
20 PRINT
25 FOR K=1 TO 20 STEP 1
30 READ N$,X$,D$,F$
35 IF F$ = " 4A " THEN 45
40 GO TO 50
45 PRINT N$,X$,D$
50 NEXT K
55 STOP
101 DATA "JOHN WILLIAMS "," M "," 21/05/62 "," 4C "
102 DATA "CHERYL SMITH "," F "," 05/02/62 "," 4A "
103 DATA "DANIEL JAMES "," M "," 13/11/61 "," 4B "
104 DATA "ADRIAN ELLIOT "," M "," 14/09/61 "," 4A "
105 DATA "SUSAN EVANS "," F "," 03/02/62 "," 4C "
106 DATA "PETER JOHNSON "," M "," 21/12/61 "," 4B "
107 DATA "JANE KEMP "," F "," 14/04/62 "," 4B "
108 DATA "ANN STEVENS "," F "," 30/11/61 "," 4C "
109 DATA "FREDERICK LEE "," M "," 12/10/61 "," 4A "
110 DATA "JILL DEVONPORT"," F "," 02/01/62 "," 4C "
111 DATA "CATHY WILSON "," F "," 19/04/62 "," 4B "
112 DATA "ALISON FRANCIS"," F "," 07/10/61 "," 4A "
113 DATA "DAVID JACOBS "," M "," 04/03/62 "," 4A "
114 DATA "JOAN SIMPSON "," F "," 10/09/61 "," 4C "
115 DATA "BRIAN JACKSON "," M "," 14/12/61 "," 4B "
116 DATA "GRAHAM MURPHY "," M "," 07/08/62 "," 4C "
117 DATA "JULIA DAWSON "," F "," 24/07/62 "," 4A "
118 DATA "JOHN ADAMSON "," M "," 15/05/62 "," 4B "
119 DATA "SYLVIA MEAD "," F "," 08/12/61 "," 4C "
120 DATA "JUDITH WEST "," F "," 01/02/62 "," 4B "
200 END
*
```

Results

```
FORM 4A

NAME          SEX        DATE OF BIRTH

CHERYL SMITH   F          05/02/62
ADRIAN ELLIOT  M          14/09/61
FREDERICK LEE  M          12/10/61
ALISON FRANCIS F          07/10/61
DAVID JACOBS   M          04/03/62
JULIA DAWSON   F          24/07/62
```

Points to notice

● The data lines have been numbered 101 to 120 for convenience of counting, and also so that they can be used in other programs.

● The arrangement of IF and GO TO statements does not follow the flow diagram exactly.

● A certain amount of space (called a *field*) is allowed for each data item. This makes the data easier to read. However the same spaces *must* be included in references to the data (such as statement 35).

Example 7A2

An index of farms in a certain area is kept by a county council. The information for each farm is:

NAME, OWNER'S NAME, NUMBER OF ACRES, CATEGORY

The categories are:

DAIRY, CEREAL, VEGETABLE, MIXED.

Write a program to read the name of a category, then read ten sets of information. Print the name, owner's name and number of acres of the farms in that category.

Method

The category chosen is read as the variable C$.

For each farm, information is read into the variables N$ (name), O$ (owner's name), A (number of acres ordinary variable) and K$ (category).

The condition for printing the information is:

Is C$ = K$?

If so, N$, O$ and A are printed.

Flow diagram

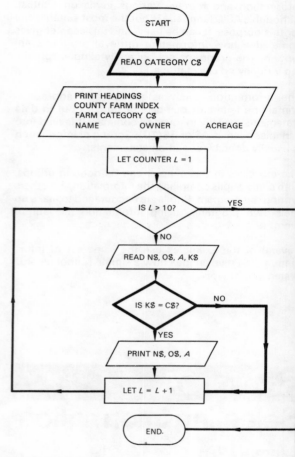

Variables

C$: category to be printed
L: counter (1 to 10)   N$: farm name
O$: owner's name   A: number of acres
K$: farm category

Program

```
5 READ C$
10 PRINT "COUNTY FARM INDEX"
15 PRINT
20 PRINT "CATEGORY : ";C$
25 PRINT
30 PRINT "NAME","OWNER","ARCREAGE"
35 PRINT
40 FOR L=1 TO 10 STEP 1
45 READ N$,O$,A,K$
50 IF K$=C$ THEN 60
55 GO TO 65
60 PRINT N$,O$,A
65 NEXT L
70 STOP
100 DATA "DAIRY"
101 DATA "ELMWAY     ","A.J.ROBERTS ",21,"CEREAL"
102 DATA "FOURFIELDS","K.JACKSON  ",17,"DAIRY"
103 DATA "KINGSTON  ","S.M.SWANN  ",42,"DAIRY"
104 DATA "HILLEND   ","P.STEVENSON",18,"MIXED"
105 DATA "RIVERSIDE ","K.S.WATERS ",13,"VEGETABLE"
106 DATA "MILL FARM ","A.OWEN     ",33,"CEREAL"
107 DATA "FERNDALE  ","M.HUNTER   ",29,"DAIRY"
108 DATA "PINETOWN  ","H.MULLER   ",52,"CEREAL"
109 DATA "GLEN GRANT","B.GRANT    ",18,"VEGETABLE"
110 DATA "PORTERFORD","Y.DARCY    ",34,"MIXED"
200 END
*
```

Results

```
COUNTY FARM INDEX

CATEGORY : DAIRY

NAME         OWNER        ARCREAGE

FOURFIELDS   K.JACKSON    17
KINGSTON     S.M.SWANN    42
FERNDALE     M.HUNTER     29
```

Points to notice

● For a different category to be printed, only statement 100 need be changed.

● Fields of a certain width are used for the name and the owner's name.

Exercise 7A

Copy and complete the flow diagram and program for this problem:

1. Make up a list of 20 English words and their meanings in French. Put this information in data statements such as this:

101 DATA "DAY", "JOUR"

Write a program to read one English word, and then the 20 translation data statements. If the English word is in the list, the corresponding French word is printed. Otherwise the message WORD NOT IN LIST is printed.

Method

Suitable variables are:

W$: English word to be translated
E$: English word in translation statement
F$: French word in translation statement

The variable W$ is read first. A loop (counter K from 1 to 20) reads the variables E$ and F$ from each data statement. The condition

Is W$=E$?

selects the required English word. When found, the French word F$ is printed, and the program stops.

If the end of the loop is reached without the word being found, the message WORD NOT IN LIST is printed.

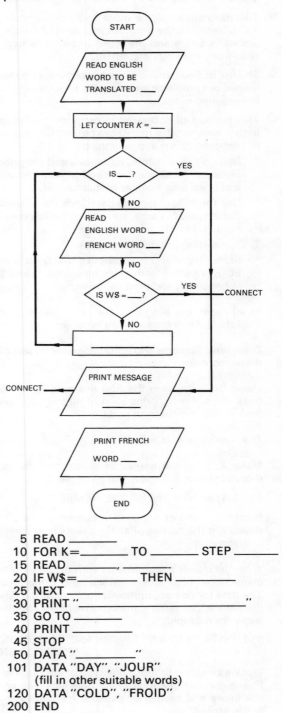

```
  5 READ _____
 10 FOR K=_____ TO _____ STEP _____
 15 READ _____, _____
 20 IF W$=_____ THEN _____
 25 NEXT _____
 30 PRINT "_____"
 35 GO TO _____
 40 PRINT _____
 45 STOP
 50 DATA "_____"
101 DATA "DAY", "JOUR"
    (fill in other suitable words)
120 DATA "COLD", "FROID"
200 END
```

Points to notice

● With only two changes, this program could find the English meaning of a French word.

● This program would be most useful on a micro-computer, with the program and pairs of words stored in a file, and the word to be translated read from an INPUT statement.

● The list of English and French words can be much longer, but problems arise over the time taken to find the required word.

● This method of accessing information (using one item as a *key* to other items) can be used for a number of purposes. Some suggestions are:

  ● Store a list of names, addresses and telephone numbers. Read one name and print the address and telephone number of that person.

  ● Use the school records data from the example. Read a pupil's name, and print his or her date of birth and form.

  ● Translation to other languages.

  ● Store a list of abbreviations like NATO, IBM and ECG, together with their meanings. Read an abbreviation and print its meaning.

In all cases the programs are very similar to the English-to-French translation program.

Draw flow diagrams and write programs for some of these problems:

2. Using the data from the first example, or similar ones of your own, print a list of all the girls, with their name, date of birth and form.

The condition is: Is X $=$"F"?

3. Make a list of the names of plants and the best month for planting them. For example:

102 DATA "HYACINTH", "SEPTEMBER"

Input the name of a month, and then all the plant data. Print the names of all the plants best planted in that month.

4. A dentist makes appointments with his patients for inspections, fillings, extractions, and other work. The data for one appointment consists of the time, the patient's name, and the purpose of the appointment, for example:

111 DATA "9.15 A.M.", "MRS A. C. EDMUNDS", "INSPECTION"

Write a program to input one type of appointment, then a number of appointment data sets, and print the times and names of patients for that type of appointment.

5. A list of the examination results of 20 candidates in a subject is put on data cards. Each card contains a name, candidate number and grade (A, B, C, D or E). Read the cards, and print the name and candidate number of those with grade A.

☐ 6. Use a local newspaper to make a list of the following information for twelve houses which are for sale:

type of house, area, estate agent, price

A typical data set is:

103 DATA "SEMI-DETACHED", "BECCLES", "NORTHFIELD PROPERTIES", 8300

The price is an ordinary variable, not in inverted commas.

Write one (or more) of the following programs:

(a) Print a list of all the information for the houses with prices less than £7500.
(b) Print a list of all the information for the terraced houses.
(c) Read the name of an area, and print a list of all the information for the houses in that area.
(d) Read the name of an estate agent and print a list of all the information for the houses he has for sale.

Section 7B
Sorting information with more than one condition

Example 7B1

Using the information from the previous example (the name, sex, date of birth and form of 20 fourth year pupils) print a list of the names and dates of birth of all the boys in form 4C:

Method

Here there are two conditions:

Is X$=$"M" *and*
Is F$=$"4C"?

The condition statements must be linked up so that the name and date of birth are printed if the answer to *both* questions is yes.

Flow diagram

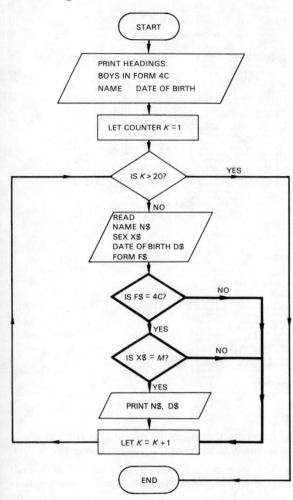

START

PRINT HEADINGS:
BOYS IN FORM 4C
NAME   DATE OF BIRTH

LET COUNTER K = 1

IS K > 20? —— YES

NO

READ
NAME N$
SEX X$
DATE OF BIRTH D$
FORM F$

IS F$ = 4C? —— NO

YES

IS X$ = M? —— NO

YES

PRINT N$, D$

LET K = K + 1

END

Variables

N$: name   X$: sex   D$: date of birth
F $: form   K: counter (1 to 20)

Program

```
5 PRINT "BOYS IN FORM 4C"
10 PRINT
15 PRINT "NAME","DATE OF BIRTH"
20 PRINT
25 FOR K=1 TO 20 STEP 1
30 READ N$,X$,D$,F$
35 IF F$ = " 4C " THEN 45
40 GO TO 60
45 IF X$=" M " THEN 55
50 GO TO 60
55 PRINT N$,D$
60 NEXT K
65 STOP
101 DATA "JOHN WILLIAMS  " , " M " , " 21/05/62 " , " 4C "
102 DATA "CHERYL SMITH   " , " F " , " 05/02/62 " , " 4A "
103 DATA "DANIEL JAMES   " , " M " , " 13/11/61 " , " 4B "
104 DATA "ADRIAN ELLIOT  " , " M " , " 14/09/61 " , " 4A "
105 DATA "SUSAN EVANS    " , " F " , " 03/02/62 " , " 4C "
106 DATA "PETER JOHNSON  " , " M " , " 21/12/61 " , " 4B "
107 DATA "JANE KEMP      " , " F " , " 14/04/62 " , " 4B "
108 DATA "ANN STEVENS    " , " F " , " 30/11/61 " , " 4C "
109 DATA "FREDERICK LEE  " , " M " , " 12/10/61 " , " 4A "
110 DATA "JILL DEVONPORT" , " F " , " 02/01/62 " , " 4C "
111 DATA "CATHY WILSON   " , " F " , " 19/04/62 " , " 4B "
112 DATA "ALISON FRANCIS" , " F " , " 07/10/61 " , " 4A "
113 DATA "DAVID JACOBS   " , " M " , " 04/03/62 " , " 4A "
114 DATA "JOAN SIMPSON   " , " F " , " 10/09/61 " , " 4C "
115 DATA "BRIAN JACKSON  " , " M " , " 14/12/61 " , " 4B "
116 DATA "GRAHAM MURPHY  " , " M " , " 07/08/62 " , " 4C "
117 DATA "JULIA DAWSON   " , " F " , " 24/07/62 " , " 4A "
118 DATA "JOHN ADAMSON   " , " M " , " 15/05/62 " , " 4B "
119 DATA "SYLVIA MEAD    " , " F " , " 08/12/61 " , " 4C "
120 DATA "JUDITH WEST    " , " F " , " 01/02/62 " , " 4B "
200 END
*
```

Results

```
BOYS IN FORM 4C

NAME            DATE OF BIRTH

JOHN WILLIAMS   21/05/62
GRAHAM MURPHY   07/08/62
```

Points to notice

● Notice carefully how the IF and GO TO statements are connected (statements 35 to 50).

● This is a program where information is printed where one condition AND another condition are satisfied.

Example 7B2

Using the information from the previous example (the name, sex, date of birth and form of 20 fourth year pupils), print a list of the name and date of birth of all the pupils in form 4A or 4B.

Method

Again there are two conditions:

Is F$="4A"?   or
Is F$="4B"?

The condition statements must be linked up so that the name and date of birth are printed if the answer to *either* question is yes.

Flow diagram

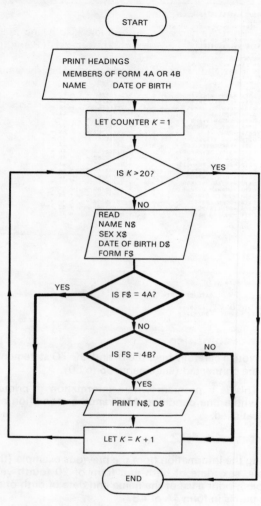

START

PRINT HEADINGS
MEMBERS OF FORM 4A OR 4B
NAME   DATE OF BIRTH

LET COUNTER K = 1

IS K > 20? —— YES

NO

READ
NAME N$
SEX X$
DATE OF BIRTH D$
FORM F$

YES

IS F$ = 4A?

NO

IS FS = 4B? —— NO

YES

PRINT N$, D$

LET K = K + 1

END

Variables

N$: name   X$: sex   D$: date of birth
F$: form   K: counter (1 to 20)

Program

```
5 PRINT "MEMBERS OF FORMS 4A OR 4B"
10 PRINT
15 PRINT "NAME","DATE OF BIRTH"
20 PRINT
25 FOR K=1 TO 20 STEP 1
30 READ N$,X$,D$,F$
35 IF F$ = " 4A " THEN 50
40 IF F$ = " 4B " THEN 50
45 GO TO 55
50 PRINT N$,D$
55 NEXT K
60 STOP
101 DATA "JOHN WILLIAMS  ", " M ", " 21/05/62 ", " 4C "
102 DATA "CHERYL SMITH   ", " F ", " 05/02/62 ", " 4A "
103 DATA "DANIEL JAMES   ", " M ", " 13/11/61 ", " 4B "
104 DATA "ADRIAN ELLIOT  ", " M ", " 14/09/61 ", " 4A "
105 DATA "SUSAN EVANS    ", " F ", " 03/02/62 ", " 4C "
106 DATA "PETER JOHNSON  ", " M ", " 21/12/61 ", " 4B "
107 DATA "JANE KEMP      ", " F ", " 14/04/62 ", " 4B "
108 DATA "ANN STEVENS    ", " F ", " 30/11/61 ", " 4C "
109 DATA "FREDERICK LEE  ", " M ", " 12/10/61 ", " 4A "
110 DATA "JILL DEVONPORT", " F ", " 02/01/62 ", " 4C "
111 DATA "CATHY WILSON   ", " F ", " 19/04/62 ", " 4B "
112 DATA "ALISON FRANCIS", " F ", " 07/10/61 ", " 4A "
113 DATA "DAVID JACOBS   ", " M ", " 04/03/62 ", " 4A "
114 DATA "JOAN SIMPSON   ", " F ", " 10/09/61 ", " 4C "
115 DATA "BRIAN JACKSON  ", " M ", " 14/12/61 ", " 4B "
116 DATA "GRAHAM MURPHY  ", " M ", " 07/08/92 ", " 4C "
117 DATA "JULIA DAWSON   ", " F ", " 24/07/62 ", " 4A "
118 DATA "JOHN ADAMSON   ", " M ", " 15/05/62 ", " 4B "
119 DATA "SYLVIA MEAD    ", " F ", " 08/12/61 ", " 4C "
120 DATA "JUDITH WEST    ", " F ", " 01/02/62 ", " 4B "
200 END
*
```

Results

```
MEMBERS OF FORMS 4A OR 4B

NAME            DATE OF BIRTH

CHERYL SMITH    05/02/62
DANIEL JAMES    13/11/61
ADRIAN ELLIOT   14/09/61
PETER JOHNSON   21/12/61
JANE KEMP       14/04/62
FREDERICK LEE   12/10/61
CATHY WILSON    19/04/62
ALISON FRANCIS  07/10/61
DAVID JACOBS    04/03/62
BRIAN JACKSON   14/12/61
JULIA DAWSON    24/07/62
JOHN ADAMSON    15/05/62
JUDITH WEST     01/02/62
```

Points to notice

● Compare the layout of the IF and GO TO statements with those of the previous program.

● This is a program where information is printed where one condition OR another condition is satisfied.

Exercise 7B

Draw flow diagrams and write programs for some of these problems:

1. Using the information from the school examples, print a list of the names and dates of birth of the girls in form 4A.

   The conditions are:

   Is F$="4A"?   and
   Is X$="F"?

□ 2. Print a list of the names and dates of birth of the members of form 4B, with all the girls first and all the boys afterwards.

   The data must be read twice, using a RESTORE statement. The conditions for the first loop are:

Is F$="4B"?
and X$="F"?

and in the second loop:

Is F$="4B"?
and X$="M"?

3. At a maternity hospital, records are kept of women with children. Each record contains a name, address, age (years only) and number of children. A typical record would be:

105 DATA "F. M. EVANS", "37 OAK AVENUE,
                        BRAMPTON", 26, 2

The age and number of children are read as ordinary variables, without dollar signs.

Make a list of fifteen such records, and write programs to read this information and print:

(a) The names, addresses and numbers of children of all the women less than 20 years old.
(b) The names, addresses and ages of all the women with 4 or more children.
(c) The names, addresses, ages and numbers of children of all the women under 25 with more than two children.

If one program is written to do all three questions, there must be RESTORE statements between different parts.

4. Make a list of names and three sports played by members of your form. If a person plays less than three sports, write NONE to make up three. A typical data set is:

107 DATA "SUSAN SMYTHE", "TENNIS",
                       "HOCKEY", "NONE"

Write either or both of these programs, using this information:

(a) Print a list of the names of all the people who play football.

There are three variables for the sports, say T$, U$, V$.

The conditions are:

Is T$="FOOTBALL"?   or
Is U$="FOOTBALL"?   or
Is V$="FOOTBALL"?

(b) Read the name of a sport and print a list of the names of the pupils who play it.

5. Compile a list of the following information for ten types of car:

NAME   PRICE (£)   ENGINE CAPACITY (CC)
FUEL CONSUMPTION (MPG)
TOP SPEED (MPH)

Use a literal variable for the name, and ordinary variables for the other items. Write one or more of the following programs:

(a) Print the name, price, engine capacity and fuel consumption of the cars with a top speed of 85 mph or more.
(b) Print the name, price and top speed of the cars with a fuel consumption better (more miles per gallon) than 35 mpg.
(c) Print the names of any cars with an engine capacity more than 2000 cc and price less than £3500.

Section 7C
Sorting information into categories

Example 7C

The results of an O level examination contain the name, candidate number and grade (A, B, C, D, E or U for ungraded) of each of sixteen candidates. Print a list of the name and candidate number of the candidates in each grade.

Method

A list G$(6) is used to store the names of the grades. A loop is used to work through the grades one by one. For each grade, an inner nested loop reads the list of candidates, and prints the required information for those in that grade. A RESTORE statement starts at the beginning of the list for the next grade.

Flow diagram

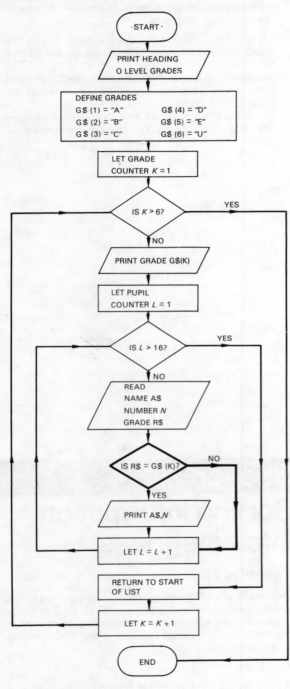

Variables

G$(6): category grades
K: grade counter (1 to 6)
L: pupil counter (1 to 16)   A$: pupil name
N: candidate number   R$: pupil grade

Program

```
2 PAGE
5 DIM G$(6)
10 PRINT "O LEVEL RESULTS"
15 PRINT, "NAME", "CANDIATE NUMBER"
20 LET G$(1)="A"
25 LET G$(2)="B"
30 LET G$(3)="C"
35 LET G$(4)="D"
40 LET G$(5)="E"
45 LET G$(6)="U"
50 FOR K=1 TO 6 STEP 1
55 PRINT
60 PRINT "GRADE : ";G$(K)
65 PRINT
70 FOR L=1 TO 16 STEP 1
75 READ A$,N,R$
80 IF R$=G$(K) THEN 90
85 GO TO 95
90 PRINT ,A$,N
95 NEXT L
100 RESTORE
105 NEXT K
110 STOP
201 DATA "JOHN BLANKE     ",3772,"C"
202 DATA "FRANK JACKSON   ",2917,"C"
203 DATA "SUSAN PALMER    ",1992,"B"
204 DATA "ANDREW EDWARDS",2374,"D"
205 DATA "MICHAEL PORTER  ",3165,"C"
206 DATA "JEAN SMITH      ",4116,"E"
207 DATA "DEBORAH ATKIN   ",1317,"A"
208 DATA "SHARON SEWELL   ",1915,"C"
209 DATA "STEVEN LONG     ",1149,"B"
210 DATA "JAMES MASON     ",4061,"C"
211 DATA "JUDITH WASE     ",3715,"U"
212 DATA "ANN MARTIN      ",2653,"C"
213 DATA "JONATHAN EVANS ",1313,"B"
214 DATA "ANDREW HODSON  ",0633,"D"
215 DATA "PAMELA BARNES   ",3161,"B"
216 DATA "CHRISTINE BELL  ",1243,"C"
300 END
*
```

Results

O LEVEL RESULTS	NAME	CANDIDATE NUMBER
GRADE : A		
	DEBORAH ATKIN	1317
GRADE : B		
	SUSAN PALMER	1992
	STEVEN LONG	1149
	JONATHAN EVANS	1313
	PAMELA BARNES	3161
GARDE : C		
	JOHN BLANKE	3772
	FRANK JACKSON	2917
	MICHAEL PORTER	3165
	SHARON SEWELL	1915
	JAMES MASON	4061
	ANN MARTIN	2653
	CHRISTINE BELL	1243
GRADE : D		
	ANDREW EDWARDS	2374
	ANDREW HODSON	633
GRADE : E		
	JEAN SMTIH	4116
GRADE : U		
	JUDITH WASE	3715

Points to notice

● The commas at the beginning of PRINT statements
15 and 90 start the output from these statements in
the second column.

Exercise 7C

Draw flow diagrams and write programs for some of
these problems:

1. Using the information from the previous examples
(the pupil form lists), print a list of the name, sex and
date of birth of the pupils in each form.

2. Use the information from Exercise 7B, Question 3,
to print a list of the names and addresses of the

women with one child, then those with two children, etc.

3. At a hospital, records are kept of blood donors, each file containing a name, donor number, address, date of birth, blood group (A, B, AB, O or R for rare) and rhesus factor (+ or −). A typical record is:

119 DATA "J. M. MARTIN", 63015, "3 LEIGH
    STREET, OXFORD", "31/08/43", "AB", "+"

Read the records of 20 donors, and print a list of the name, donor number, address, date of birth and rhesus factor of the donors in each blood group.

4. Use a railway timetable to find out the following information for (say) 20 trains departing from your local station.

TIME OF DEPARTURE   DESTINATION
TIME OF ARRIVAL

A typical data card is:

111 DATA 0940, "NORWICH", 1035

Put the names of the different destinations in a list, and then print the departure and arrival times for the trains for each destination in turn.

5. Use a copy of *TV Times* or *Radio Times* to compile a list of the following information for (say) 25 television programs:

TITLE, DAY, TIME, CHANNEL, TYPE

e.g.
113 DATA "MATCH OF THE DAY",
    "SATURDAY", 1915, "BBC1", "SPORT"

Types are:

NEWS, DOCUMENTARY, ENTERTAINMENT, SPORT

Print a list of the title, day, time and channel of the programs of each type.

Exercise 7D

1. Using the information on blood donors from Exercise 7C, write a program which reads a blood group and rhesus factor, then reads the list of donors, and prints the names and addresses of all donors with that blood group and rhesus factor.

2. Make a list of your school lessons, with the following information:

SUBJECT, DAY, PERIOD NUMBER, ROOM NUMBER

e.g.
117 DATA "PHYSICS", "TUESDAY", 3, "L4"

For each subject in turn, make a list of the day, period number and room number of the lessons in that subject.

3. At a bank, the following information is kept on people with accounts:

NAME, ADDRESS, ACCOUNT NUMBER, CREDIT LIMIT

e.g.
131 DATA "M. J. BROWN", "14 THE AVENUE,
    DOVER", 131216, 500

The account number and credit limit are ordinary variables, without inverted commas.

Make up ten such sets of data, and write a program to read the data, and print lists of the names, addresses and account numbers of people

(a) with credit limit more than £500
(b) with credit limit less than or equal to £500

4. Rewrite this program, correcting all the mistakes:

```
05  REMARK "PROGRAM TO PRINT A LIST OF
                              WORKERS
10  REMARK "WITH SALARIES OVER £3000
15  PRINT "NAME" "WORKS NUMBER
20  FOR K=1 TO 20, STEP 1
25  READ N$; W$; S
35  IF S>£3000, THEN 40
35  PRINT N$, W
40  NEXT S
45  STOP
45  DATA "A. G. BARNES", 3167, £4200.
55  DATA "J. M. STEVENS", 5112, £2913.
                              . . . etc.
100  END.
```

5. To what extent do you think that storing information (particularly concerning people) on computers can be harmful?

Write an essay giving your views on this subject, including any example where, in your opinion, computerized information storage is being, or could be, abused. Say who you think should have access to various kinds of information, and how it should be protected.

8. Functions

In BASIC language, the computer is automatically programmed to work out the values of several common functions. The integer function INT and tabulating function TAB have already been introduced. The list shows more of the functions which are available. The variable in the brackets, called the *argument* of the function, must have been read or calculated before the statement containing the function is reached.

The functions which will be introduced are of two types: general and trigonometrical. The general ones are in the first section, the trigonometrical ones are in the second.

Section 8A
General functions

Function	Description	Limits on argument
ABS(X)	gives the size of X, not counting the sign, i.e. if $X=-2$, $ABS(X)=2$	any X
INT(X)	gives whole number part of X.	any X
RND(X)	gives a random number between 0 and 1	if $X=0$, a sequence of random numbers is produced if $X>0$, the same random number is produced for the same X
SGN(X)	$=+1$ if X is positive $=-1$ if X is negative $=0$ if $X=0$	any X
SQR(X)	gives square root of X	$X\geqslant 0$
TAB(X)	tabulating function: skips X spaces before printing.	X between 0 and 120

Note: The RND function works differently on different types of computer.

Example 8A1

Print a table of 100 random integers between 1 and 10 in a table of 10 rows of 10 numbers.

Method

The function RND(0) gives a sequence of random numbers between 0 and 1, all numbers being equally likely to occur. Multiplying these by 10 gives numbers in the range 0 to 10, including fractions. Taking the whole number part gives integers from 0 to 9, and adding 1 gives integers from 1 to 10. Thus the calculation statement is

LET X=INT (10∗RND(0))+1

In order that a different sequence of random numbers is produced each time the program is run, a number K is read, and the quantity $D=RND(K)$ calculated, but not printed. This sets the random number generator at a different place for different values of K.

Nested loops are used to produce the rows and columns of the table, the column counter being innermost. A column is printed every ten spaces, starting ten spaces from the left.

Flow diagram

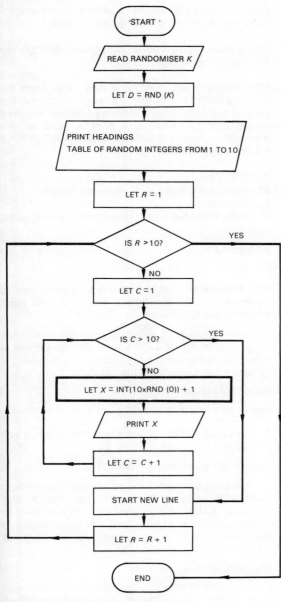

Variables

K: input number to start random sequence
D: initial random number
R: row counter (1 to 10)
C: column counter (1 to 10)
X: random integer between 1 and 10

Program

```
5   READ K
10  LET D=RND(K)
15  PRINT "TABLE OF RANDOM INTEGERS FROM 1 TO 10"
20  PRINT
25  FOR R=1 TO 10 STEP 1
30  FOR C=1 TO 10 STEP 1
35  LET X=INT(10*RND(0))+1
40  PRINT TAB(10*C);X;
45  NEXT C
50  PRINT
55  NEXT R
60  STOP
65  DATA 22
70  END
*
```

Results

```
TABLE OF RANDOM INTEGERS FROM 1 TO 10

9    9    7    7    5    7    7    2    9    4
3    5    2    10   9    2    1    8    10   4
5    10   8    3    1    10   10   5    9    5
7    10   9    7    9    10   3    10   7    1
8    3    5    1    4    8    6    10   1    3
7    9    7    7    5    2    7    7    2    1
6    3    10   4    9    1    8    7    8    6
6    5    5    6    8    6    4    9    7    ·8
6    6    4    6    10   10   8    8    8    8
5    5    10   2    3    6    6    3    9    1
```

Points to notice

● The TAB function in line 40 gives a column every ten spaces, starting ten spaces from the left.

Example 8A2

The sugar content of a certain soft drink is supposed to be 7%. If the percentage for a sample from a batch is within ·2% of 7%, then the batch is accepted, otherwise it is rejected.

Write a program to read a batch number, weight of sugar (grams) and total sample weight (grams), work out the percentage of sugar, and print a message REJECT if this differs from 7% by more than ·2%. Otherwise print a message ACCEPT.

Method

The percentage of sugar is

$$P = \frac{S}{W} \times 100$$

P: percentage sugar S: weight of sugar
W: sample weight B: batch number

The difference between this and 7% is

$$D = 7 - P$$

D: difference

The sample is rejected if the size of this difference, not counting sign, is more than ·2.
The condition is:

Is $ABS(D) > ·2$?

Flow diagram

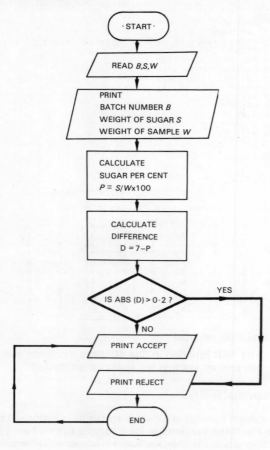

Program

```
 5 READ B,S,W
10 PRINT "BATCH NUMBER : ";B
15 PRINT "WEIGHT OF SUGAR : ";S;" GM"
20 PRINT "WEIGHT OF SAMPLE : ";W;" GM"
25 LET P=S/W*100
30 LET D=7-P
35 IF ABS(D)>.2 THEN 50
40 PRINT "ACCEPT"
45 GOTO 55
50 PRINT "REJECT"
55 STOP
60 DATA 1733,174.3,2500
65 END
*
```

Results

```
BATCH NUMBER :  1733
WEIGHT OF SUGAR :   174.3   GM
WEIGHT OF SAMPLE :   2500   GM
ACCEPT
```

Exercise 8A

1. Print a table of 100 random numbers (in the range 0 to 1) in five columns of 20 numbers each.

2. Print a table of 100 random integers in the range 1 to 100 set out as in Question 1.

3. Machine parts are rejected if they differ from the required length by more than a certain tolerance. For each of ten parts, read a measured length, required length and tolerance, and print a table of this information, together with the message ACCEPT or REJECT as required.

Variables

M: measured length R: required length
T: tolerance
D: difference between measured and required length

Formula

$D=M-R$

4. The probability that an electrical component is defective is 0·1. Simulate a batch of 100 such components as follows:

For each component, generate a random number X, between 0 and 1. If $X<0·1$ then the component is defective, otherwise not. Count the number of defective components in the batch.

Modification

Use nested loops to simulate five such batches.

5. The probabilities of different types of weather at a place are:

sunny: ·3   overcast: ·6   rain: ·1

Simulate a month's weather by generating a random number W (between 0 and 1) for each day. If W is less than ·3, the weather is sunny, if W is from ·3 to ·9 the weather is overcast, and if W is more than ·9 there is rain. Print a table of the date and type of weather.

Modification

Keep a record of your local weather for a month, and work out the probabilities of the weather types from the results. Use these probabilities to simulate the month's weather, and compare the results with the actual weather record.

6. Each move of a game involving two players is as follows: each player throws a dice, and the one with the higher number scores one point (there is no score if the numbers are equal). Write a program to play this game for ten moves, adding up the score for each player. Print the output under these headings:

MOVE NO.   DICE A   DICE B   TOTAL A
                              TOTAL B

The statement for getting a random whole number from 1 to 6 is:

LET X=INT (6∗RND(0)+1)

Two conditions will be required: one to see if a move is a draw, and the other to see which player wins.

Read each player's lucky number to set the random number generator at the start.

Section 8B
Trigonometrical functions

The following trigonometrical functions are available in BASIC language:

SIN(X)	gives sine of angle X	X in radians
COS(X)	gives cosine of angle X	X in radians
TAN(X)	gives tangent of angle X	X in radians
ATN(Y)	gives the angle (in radians) having tangent Y	any value of Y

Measuring angles in radians will be unfamiliar to some. The conversion is based on

π radians=180°

i.e. 3·14159 radians=180°

In all the programs, input and output is in degrees. Conversions are made to radians only for calculation purposes.

Example 8B1

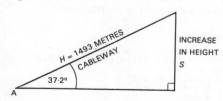

A cableway 1493 metres long slopes at 37·2° to the horizontal. Calculate its increase in height.

Method

The length S of the right-angled triangle is required, and the length H and the angle A known. From the theory of trigonometry:

$$\sin A=\frac{\text{length } S}{\text{length } H}$$

i.e. length S=length $H\times \sin A$

To change the angle to radians for the calculation:

180°=3·14159 radians
1°=3·14159÷180 radians
A°=3·14159÷180×A radians

Flow diagram

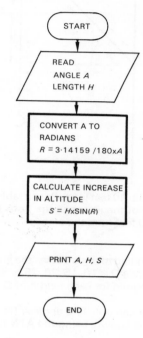

Variables

A: angle of slope of cableway (degrees)
H: length of cableway (metres)
R: angle of slope (radians)
S: increase in height (metres)

Program

```
5 READ A,H
10 LET R=3.14159/180∗A
15 LET S=H∗SIN(R)
20 PRINT "CABLEWAY ANGLE OF INCLINATION:",A;"DEGREES"
25 PRINT "LENGTH:",H;"METRES"
30 PRINT "INCREASE IN ALTITUDE:",S;"METRES"
35 STOP
40 DATA 37.2,1493
45 END
```

Results

Example 8B2

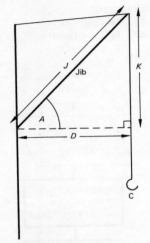

A crane has a jib 40 feet long. Print a table of the angles of inclination of the jib when the hook hangs 10, 15, 20, 25 and 30 feet from the crane.

Method
In the right-angled triangle above, the jib length J is 40 feet, the distance D is 10, 15, 20, 25 or 30 feet, and the angle A is required for each length of D.

The computer can only find angle A (in radians) if the tangent of A is known, using the ATN function.

$$\tan A = \frac{\text{distance } K}{\text{distance } D}$$

Distance K can be found using Pythagoras' theorem:

$$J^2 = D^2 + K^2$$
i.e. $K^2 = J^2 - D^2$
$$K = \sqrt{(J^2 - D^2)}$$

Then, in BASIC notation,

$A = \text{ATN } (K/D)$

The angle is changed to degrees by the equation:

$G = 180 \div 3 \cdot 14159 \times A$

G: angle in degrees

A loop is used to give D the values 10, 15, 20, 25, 30.

Flow diagram

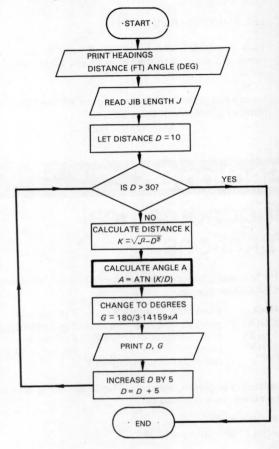

Variables
J: jib length (feet)
D: distance of hook from crane (feet)
K: working variable (feet)
A: angle of inclination of jib (radians)
G: angle of inclination of jib (degrees)

Program

```
5 PRINT "DISTANCE (FT)","ANGLE (DEGREES)"
10 READ J
15 FOR D=10 TO 30 STEP 5
20 LET K=SQR(J*J-D*D)
25 LET A=ATN(K/D)
30 LET G=180/3.14159*A
35 PRINT D,G
40 NEXT D
45 STOP
50 DATA 40
55 END
*
```

Results

DISTANCE (FT)	ANGLE (DEGREES)
10	75.5226
15	67.9757
20	60.0001
25	51.3179
30	41.4097

Exercise 8B

1. Print a table of sines, cosines and tangents of angles from 0° to 90° in steps of 1°.

2. Read the co-ordinates of a point P, and calculate its distance D from the origin O, and the angle A between D and the x axis.

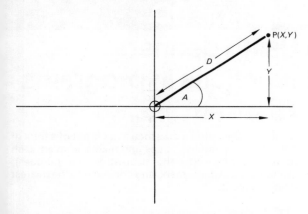

3. Read the distance D of a point P from the origin O, and the angle A that D makes with the x axis. Calculate the x and y co-ordinates of P.

4. Read the angle of climb and distance flown of an aeroplane, and calculate its increase in altitude.

5. The angle of elevation of the top of a mountain from a point 12·63 km away, at sea level, is 13·78°. Calculate the height of the mountain.

6.

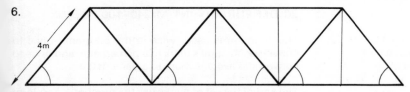

Calculate the total length of all the beams in this structure. All angles marked are 53·6°, all diagonal beams are 4 metres.

7. A shell is fired from a gun with a speed V m/s, at an angle A to the horizontal. The distance it travels before retunring to the ground (its range) is worked out by the formula:

$$R = \frac{V^2}{G} \sin 2A$$

V: speed on firing (m/s)
G: acceleration due to gravity (9·8 m/s²)
A: angle of firing (radians) R: range (m)

Read a value of speed V (usually between 500 and 1000 m/s) and print a table of ranges for angles A from 10° to 80° in steps of 5°.

8. The maximum height reached by the shell in Question 7 is:

$$H = \frac{V^2}{2G} (\sin A)^2$$

H: maximum height (m)
(other letters as before)

Print a table of these heights for speeds and angles as in Question 7.

9. The sketch shows a swing bridge in its open position. Calculate the angle that the road sections make with the horizontal (variable A) and the speed (in degrees per second) at which the sections must rotate for the bridge to open in 45 seconds.

Formula

$$S = \frac{A}{45}$$

S: speed (degrees per second) A: angle (degrees)

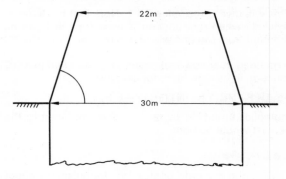

Section 8C
Defined functions

In addition to the standard function in BASIC language, it is possible to define functions in a program, which can then be used as often as necessary during that program.

The defining statement contains:

● the word DEF

● the function name, consisting of the letters FN followed by the letter identifying the function

● a variable (in brackets), called the *argument*, used in calculating the function

● the formula for working out the function, using the argument.

For example,

10 DEF FNT(X)=10∗X

makes function FNT produce a number ten times the argument. It may be used later in the program, as follows:

35 LET A=3·71
40 LET C=FNT(A)

This will give C the value 37·1. Note that the letter in brackets when the function is used (line 40) can be different from the one where it is defined (line 10).

A defined function may contain a standard BASIC function in its definition, for example:

15 DEF FNR(Y)=INT(10∗Y+0·5)

multiplies a number by ten and then rounds it to the nearest whole number.

Exercise 8C

1. Describe in words, or algebraic formulae, the effect of the following functions:

   (a) 10 DEF FNP(Y)=100−Y
   (b) 15 DEF FNQ(X)=3∗X∗X−2∗X+17
   (c) 20 DEF FNR(A)=INT(10∗RND(A)+1)
   (d) 25 DEF FNS(M)=SQR(1−M∗M)
   (e) 30 DEF FNT(K)=(K+1)/(K−1)

2. Two of the above functions will give errors if their arguments have certain values. Which functions are they, and what values are not permitted?

3. In the above functions:

   (a) If $K=47$, what is FNP(K)?
   (b) If $Y=2$, what is FNQ(Y)?
   (c) If $M=3$, what values can FNR(M) have?
   (d) If $L=0·6$, what is FNS(L)?
   (e) If $S=0·5$, what is FNT(S)?

Section 8D
Using defined functions in programs

Example 8D1

A set of examination marks for a class is out of a total of 240. Read the pupils' names and marks, convert each to a percentage (to the nearest whole number), calculate the average mark, and convert it to the nearest whole percent.

Method

The formula for converting a mark out of 240 to a percentage is:

$$P=\frac{M}{240}\times 100$$

P: percentage M: mark

Adding 0·5 and taking the integer part rounds to the nearest whole number.

The function in BASIC notation is:

20 DEF FNR(M)=INT(M/240∗100+0·5)

This function is used twice in the program—once to convert each pupil's mark to a percentage, and once to convert the average mark to a percentage.

The end of the set of marks has the number −1. A loop is formed by condition statements to work through the marks. There is a counter to record the number of pupils.

Flow diagram

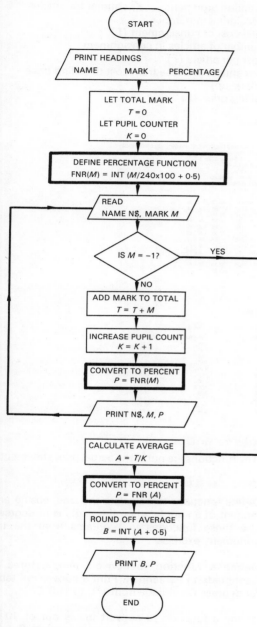

Variables

T: total mark K: pupil counter
$N\$$: pupil name M: mark
P: percentage A: average
B: average to nearest whole number

Program

```
5 PRINT "NAME","MARK","PERCENTAGE"
10 LET T=0
15 LET K=0
20 DEF FNR(M)=INT(M/240*100+0.5)
25 READ N$,M
30 IF M=-1 THEN 60
35 LET T=T+M
40 LET K=K+1
45 LET P=FNR(M)
50 PRINT N$,M,P
55 GO TO 25
60 LET A=T/K
65 LET B=INT(A+0.5)
70 LET P=FNR(A)
75 PRINT "AVERAGE",B,P
80 STOP
85 DATA "JOAN WILLIAMS",179
90 DATA "ANGELA CARTER",113
95 DATA "BRIAN GIBSON",211
100 DATA "DENISE ELSE",154
105 DATA "JOHN BAXTER",163
110 DATA "ELAINE SUMMERS",201
115 DATA "XXX",-1
120 END
*
```

Results

NAME	MARK	PERCENTAGE
JOAN WILLIAMS	179	75
ANGELA CARTER	113	47
BRIAN GIBSON	211	88
DENISE ELSE	154	64
JOHN BAXTER	163	68
ELAINE SUMMERS	201	84
AVERAGE	170	71

Points to notice

● The last data card must have a dummy name before the −1.

● The pupil counter K must start at 0.

Example 8D2

In many calculations concerning money, answers must be rounded to the nearest whole number of pence, e.g.: £371·4285 rounds to £371·43.

To achieve this, the sum of money must first be multiplied by 100, to change it to pence, then rounded to the nearest whole number (·5 added and the integer part taken), then divided by 100 to change it back to pounds. The function is defined by:

10 DEF FNP(M)=INT(M*100+0·5)/100

M: sum of money (£)

A use for this function is in the following example:

At a clothes shop, the selling price of an article is calculated as follows:

The total cost of a consignment of articles, the number in the consignment, and the percentage increase from cost to selling price are read from data.

The cost price for one article is

$$C=\frac{T}{N}$$

C: cost per article (£)
T: total consignment cost (£)
N: number in consignment

The selling price for each article is

$$S=(1+\frac{P}{100})\times C$$

S: selling price P: percentage increase

The cost and selling prices are rounded to the nearest penny before printing.

Write a program to calculate the cost and selling prices of twelve articles, reading as data the total consignment costs, the numbers in the consignments, and the percentage mark-up for each.

Flow diagram

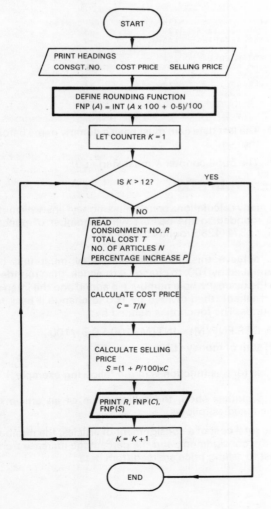

START

PRINT HEADINGS
CONSGT. NO.   COST PRICE   SELLING PRICE

DEFINE ROUNDING FUNCTION
FNP (A) = INT (A × 100 + 0·5)/100

LET COUNTER K = 1

IS K > 12?   —YES→

NO

READ
CONSIGNMENT NO. R
TOTAL COST T
NO. OF ARTICLES N
PERCENTAGE INCREASE P

CALCULATE COST PRICE
C = T/N

CALCULATE SELLING
PRICE
S = (1 + P/100)×C

PRINT R, FNP (C),
FNP (S)

K = K + 1

END

Variables

A: function argument   K: counter for articles
R: consignment number
T: total cost of consignment (£)
N: number of articles in consignment
C: cost per article (£)
P: percentage increase from cost to selling price (mark-up)
S: selling price (£)

Program

```
5 PRINT "CONSGT.NO.","COST PRICE","SELLING PRICE"
10 DEF FNP(A)=INT(A*100+0.5)/100
15 FOR K=1 TO 12 STEP 1
20 READ R,T,N,P
25 LET C=T/N
30 LET S=(1+P/100)*C
35 PRINT R,FNP(C),FNP(S)
40 NEXT K
45 STOP
50 DATA 1413 ,  46.73 , 13 , 62
55 DATA 2048 , 107.96 , 22 , 48
60 DATA 4117 ,  23.14 ,  2 , 71
65 DATA  794 , 296.57 ,  5 , 48
70 DATA 3142 ,  79.62 , 20 , 65
75 DATA 5669 ,  33.00 ,  3 , 50
80 DATA 2049 ,  47.87 , 24 , 78
85 DATA 1522 , 117.17 ,  5 , 64
90 DATA 2050 ,  67.33 ,  8 , 70
95 DATA 1827 , 113.48 ,  9 , 54
100DATA 2336 ,  37.33 ,  2 , 64
105DATA 3047 ,  49.57 , 12 , 42
100 END
```

Results

CONSGT.NO	COST PRICE	SELLING PRICE
1413	3.59	5.82
2048	4.91	7.26
4117	11.57	19.78
794	59.31	87.78
3142	3.98	6.57
5669	11	16.5
2049	1.99	3.55
1522	23.43	38.43
2050	8.42	14.31
1827	12.61	19.42
2336	18.66	30.61
3047	4.13	5.87

Points to notice

● The functions are put in the actual print statements.

Exercise 8D

1. Define functions to calculate the sine, cosine and tangent of an angle when the angle is in degrees. Use these functions in programs from the trigonometry exercise.

2. Define a function to convert temperatures in Centigrade to Fahrenheit. Print a conversion table for degrees Centigrade from 1°C to 100°C.

3. Define a function to convert marks out of 40 to percentages, to the nearest whole number. Read a set of marks out of 40, and print a list of them, together with their corresponding percentages.

. The formula for the volume of this shape is:

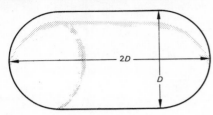

$$V = \frac{5}{12}\pi D^3$$

V: volume D: diameter π: 3·14159

Define a function to calculate the volume, and print a table of volumes for diameters from 0·2 cm to 3 cm in steps of 0·2 cm.

☐ **Modification**
Work out a formula for the surface area (the shape is a cylinder with a hemisphere on each end) and include a column for the surface area for each volume.

5. Define a function to convert German marks to English pounds, for use in the following program:

Machine parts are imported to Britain from Germany. Each consignment is accompanied by an invoice with a list of part numbers, quantities and prices (in marks). The number of different parts is shown at the top of the invoice.

Read the number of different parts, and use it in a loop of variable length to read each part number, quantity and price. Work out the cost (cost=quantity × price) and convert it to pounds. Add up the total cost in marks, and then convert it to pounds.

Print the contents of the invoice, and the totals, using the headings:

PART NO.	QUANTITY	PRICE (DM)	COST (DM)	COST (£)
...	...	...	...	...
		TOTAL:	...	...

The current rate of exchange is

£1 = DM 4·65

but this varies with time. Use an up-to-date figure.

Exercise 8E

1. The height of the tide above or below its average level is calculated from the formula:

$$D = A \times \cos(2 \times \pi \times F \times T)$$

A: maximum height above or below average (m)

F: $\dfrac{1}{12\cdot25}$ (high tide every 12·25 hours)

T: time (hours) since last high tide
D: height of the tide (m) $\pi = 3\cdot14159$

Read the time of a morning high tide (in hours and decimals of an hour: 9·50 for 9.30 a.m.), and a value of the maximum tide height A. Print a table of the height of the tide every quarter hour till the next high tide.

Use a time counter T from 0 to 12·25 in steps of 0·25. If H is the time of the high tide, then $H + T$ will be the time of day. Print a table of $H + T$ and D.

2. The length of a day (hours from sunrise to sunset) is (approximately, for Britain)

$$D = 12 - 6 \times \cos\left(\frac{2 \times \pi \times N}{365}\right)$$

D: day length (hours)
N: number of days from shortest day
$\pi = 3\cdot14159$

Print a table of day lengths every seven days for a year, starting from the shortest day. (The counter N will go from 0 to 365 in steps of 7.)

☐ 3. Packets of cornflakes are despatched in boxes containing 216, 72 or 24 packets. As much as possible of an order is packed in large (216 packet) boxes, the rest as far as possible in medium (72 packet) boxes, and the remainder in small (24 packet) boxes, the last of which may not be full.

Read a number of orders from data cards, each comprising an order number, and a number of packets. For each order, work out the number of large, medium and small boxes needed. Print a table with headings:

		BOXES:		
ORDER NO.	NO. OF PACKETS	LARGE	MEDIUM	SMALL

The number of large boxes is INT(N/216) where N is the number of packets.

Subtract the number of packets contained in this number of boxes from N before calculating the number of medium boxes. The number of medium and the number of small boxes are calculated in a similar way. If there is any remainder after calculating the number of small boxes, this number must be increased by 1.

4. The probability of a telephone call being received at an office switchboard in any minute is 0·3. Simulate 30 minutes of operation by generating a random number for each minute, and registering a call if it is 0·3 or less.

   Have a program loop for the time, running from 1 to 30, printing the time only when a call is registered. Count the total number of calls, and calculate the average number of calls per minute (average=total calls÷30).

5. Chemical fertilizer is sold for 85·731p per ton. Read a number of orders (each with order number and quantity), work out the cost (cost=quantity×85·731), convert it to pounds, reunded to the nearest penny. Print a table of order numbers, quantities and prices.

6. Rewrite this program, correcting all the mistakes:

```
 5 REM "PROGRAM TO CALCULATE THE
                          NUMBER
10 OF PAGES FOR DIFFERENT BOOKS AT 570
15 WORDS PER PAGE.
20 LET P(W)=INT(W/570)+1
15 PRINT WORDS, PAGES
25 FOR K=1 TO K=5 STEP 1
30 READ N,
35 PRINT N, P(W)
40 NEXT N
45 DATA 5717, 4233, 10, 463,
50 DATA 9347, 6116.
55 END.
```

9. BASIC summary

Statements

A program consists of a number of instructions to a computer. Each instruction forms a statement.

Line Numbers

Each statement starts with a line number. Statements are executed in order of line numbers.

Variables

A variable represents a number or literal data item. A variable representing a number is a single letter or letter followed by a single number

e.g. A   X3   are correct variables
      AB   5Y   are incorrect variables

A variable representing literal information is a single letter followed by a £ or $ sign

e.g. B£   M$ are correct literal variables
      K1£   £A   are incorrect literal variables

Numbers

Numbers may be positive or negative (no sign means positive), with or without a decimal point. The E notation is used for powers of ten.

e.g. 5   −7   +6·2313⎫ are correct
      1·3E5 (=1·3×10⁵)   ⎬ numbers
      3·21E−6 (=3·21×10⁻⁶)   ⎭

      4,371   3¾   £5·31   are incorrect numbers

The statements

READ   Reads next data number(s) or literal data item(s). Variables must be separated by commas.

          e.g. 10 READ A, X, B1, Y$

DATA   supplies data for read statements. Items must be separated by commas, literal data in inverted commas.

          e.g. 60 DATA −3, 41·5, 7,
                        "ACCOUNT 3"

          corresponds to the above read statement.

LET   Used in calculation statements. There must be an equals sign, with one variable to the left of it.

          e.g. 10 LET A=5
                15 LET Y=3*(X↑4−9)/2
                20 LET M=M−3
                              are correct

                30 LET A+1=B
                35 LET X↑2=3*Y
                40 LET M=4A+3B
                              are incorrect

          Symbols are (in order of execution):

          ( )   brackets
            ↑   powers and roots
          * /   multiply divide
          + −   add   subtract

PRINT   Prints values of variables listed, or headings. Commas are used to separate variables for wide spacing, semicolons give narrow spacing. A comma or semicolon at the end of a print statement puts the next output on the same line.

          e.g. 35 PRINT A, B, C
                40 PRINT "TOTAL:"; "£"; T
                45 PRINT "*";
                              are correct

                50 PRINT A B
                55 PRINT COST C
                              are incorrect

REM   Remark statement. It supplies information for the use of the programmer. Inverted commas are not necessary.

          e.g. 10 REM END OF INPUT
                        SEGMENT

FOR ... TO Indicates the beginning of a loop. The initial and final values, and step size, of the loop counter are shown.

          e.g. 10 FOR K=1 TO 10 STEP 1
                20 FOR M=A TO B STEP C
                30 FOR J=1 TO 5
                          (step 1 assumed)
                40 FOR I=10 TO 3 STEP −1

121

NEXT   Indicates the end of a loop. The loop counter is included.

              e.g. 50 NEXT K

RESTORE   Start again from the first data item, or the first data item of the statement specified.

              e.g. 105 RESTORE
                    110 RESTORE 150

IF . . . THEN Transfers control to the statement indicated if the condition included is true. If the condition is not true, control passes to the next statement.

              e.g. 35 IF K=3 THEN 200
                    40 IF X=Y THEN 150
                    50 IF A+B><4 * (C—D) THEN
                                            250

              The condition must contain one of the following relations:

              equals   =
              greater than   >
              greater than or equals   > =
              less than   <
              less than or equals   < =
              is not equal to   <> or ><

GO TO   Transfers control to the statement indicated.

              e.g. 75 GO TO 45

DIM   Dimension statement. It specifies a list of information to be stored as one variable. Different lists must be separated by commas.

              e.g. 10 DIM A(8), C$(6)

              This makes variable A store a list of eight numbers, and C$ a list of six literal data items.

INPUT   Used on terminals like a read statement. The data is supplied while the program is running. A data statement is not necessary, only the actual numbers are typed.

DEF FN   Defines a function. The function name is FN followed by a single letter. In brackets is a variable (the argument) followed by an equation using this variable to show how the function is worked out.

              e.g. 5 DEF FNA(K)=3*K+1

STOP   Stop execution.

END   End of program. It must be the last statement of the program.

10. Project programs

Project program 1
Landing the LEM

The lunar excursion module is 1000 m above its landing site on the moon, descending at 100 m/s, accelerating due to the moon's gravity at 2 m/s². Its mass is 2000 kg, plus 500 kg of fuel. The retro-rockets can develop up to 50 000 newtons of thrust, at which 10 kg/s of fuel are used up. At lower thrusts, proportionately less fuel is used.

The object is to simulate landing the LEM at less than 5 m/s, deciding on a value of the retro-thrust each second until touchdown.

Every second, a value of the retro-thrust is put in. The fuel used is calculated by:

$$u = \frac{f}{50000} \times 50$$

u: fuel used (kg) f: retro-thrust (N)

This is subtracted from the previous amount to get the amount of fuel left, and the current total LEM mass.

The deceleration is calculated from Newton's law of motion:

$$f = ma$$

i.e. $a = \dfrac{f}{m}$

a: deceleration (m/s²) m: current LEM mass (kg)

The nett deceleration is $a - 2$, allowing for the moon's gravity. This is also the change in speed in one second. It is subtracted from the previous speed to find the current speed, which is also the distance travelled in one second. This is subtracted from the previous altitude to find the current altitude.

For example: see table below.

If the speed is less than 5 m/s when the altitude first becomes negative, then a successful landing has been made.

If the speed is more, or the fuel runs out, then the LEM has crashed . . .

Example

Time (s)	Thrust (f)	Fuel used (u)	Fuel left	LEM mass (m)	Deceleration	Speed	Altitude
1	25 000 N	$\frac{25\,000}{50\,000} \times 50$ $= 25$ kg	$500 - 25$ $= 475$ kg	$2500 - 25$ $= 2475$ kg	$\frac{25\,000}{2475} - 2$ $= 8 \cdot 1$ m/s²	$100 - 8 \cdot 1$ $= 91 \cdot 9$ m/s	$1000 - 91 \cdot 9$ $= 908 \cdot 1$ m
2	20 000 N	$\frac{20\,000}{50\,000} \times 50$ $= 20$ kg	$475 - 20$ $= 455$ kg	$2475 - 20$ $= 2455$ kg	$\frac{20\,000}{2475} - 2$ $= 6 \cdot 2$ m/s²	$91 \cdot 9 - 6 \cdot 2$ $= 85 \cdot 7$ m/s	$908 \cdot 1 - 85 \cdot 7$ $= 822 \cdot 4$ m etc.

Project program 2
Keeping accounts

The system for keeping accounts at a shop is as follows:

When a sale is made, the following information is recorded:

ACCOUNT NUMBER, DATE, INVOICE NUMBER, AMOUNT

using the variables:

N: accunt number (1 to 15)   D$: date
I: invoice number   A: amount

A typical data card would be:

125 DATA 7, "23/03/76", 5164, 35·70

When money is received in payment of an account, the information is:

ACCOUNT NUMBER, DATE, RECEIPT NUMBER, AMOUNT

the amount being negative, for example:

134 DATA 9, "15/03/76", 7132, −417·26

Data cards for a week's business are prepared, not in any special order. In addition, a set of 15 data cards is prepared with:

ACCOUNT NUMBER, NAME,
BALANCE CARRIED FORWARD

for example:

100 DATA 5, "F. K. JENKINSON", 76·45

showing that £76·45 was owed by F. K. Jenkinson, account number 5.

Accounts are printed once a week from this data. The 15 balance cards are read first, followed by the invoice and receipt cards (together) ending with a data card with account number zero. Write a program to carry out this process, in the following steps:

1. Read the name and balance cards into the lists M$(15), B(15) where the index is the account number.

   Work through steps 2 to 6 for each account in turn (use a loop from 1 to 15):

2. Print the headings and information:

   ACCOUNT NUMBER: NAME:
   BALANCE CARRIED FORWARD:
   DATE   INVOICE/RECEIPT NUMBER
                  AMOUNT   BALANCE

3. Read all the invoice and receipt cards, selectin those with the required account number (use condition statement).

4. Add the amount of the selected invoice or receipt the balance (receipt amounts will be subtracted they are negative).

5. Print the information in the correct columns. E careful about spacing under wide headings.

6. Start at the beginning of the invoice and receipt da for the next account. If the first invoice or recei data card has statement number 120, then th statement

   RESTORE 120

   will accomplish this.

Modifications

● Include a credit limit in the header card for eac account. If this is exceeded at any stage, print message CREDIT LIMIT EXCEEDED.

● Include checks to see that account numbers a in the correct range (1 to 15).

● Include the customer's address in the accoun header card, and in the printout of the accoun

Project program 3
Sorting numbers in order

A systematic way of sorting numbers in order, whic can be very concisely programmed, is as follows:

Compare the first number with each subsequen number. If any subsequent number is larger than th first one, interchange the numbers. At the end of th series of comparisons, the largest number will be firs

Compare the second number with each subsequen number, interchanging as above. This series will en with the second largest number second.

Continuing this process as far as the second las number will put all the numbers in order.

Example

$\sqsubset$ comparison, $\sqsupset$ interchange,
input numbers: 6, 8, 3, 9

First number compared:				
⌐6⌐	⌐8	⌐8⌐	9	largest number
⌐8◄	6	6	6	now first
3	⌐3	3	3	
9	9	⌐9◄	8	

Second number compared:			
9	9	9	second largest
⌐6	⌐6⌐	8	number now
⌐3	3	3	second
8	⌐8◄	6	

Third number compared:			
9	9		numbers are
8	8		now in
⌐3⌐	6		order
⌐6◄	3		

Input the numbers into a list (say N(20) for 20 numbers). Use a loop (counter K from 1 to 19) to select each number in turn, and an inner nested loop (counter L from K+1 to 20) to compare the subsequent numbers.

If the numbers must be interchanged, three statements are needed, using a temporary variable X:

```
50 LET X=N(K)
55 LET N(K)=N(L)
60 LET N(L)=X
```

Number sorting is seldom used on its own. For example this sorting program can be modified to input a list of pupils' names and examination percentages, and output this data in order of percentages.

The names are stored in the list N$(20), and the percentages in P(20), in corresponding order P(10) is the percentage of the pupil whose name is in N(10).

The percentages are compared as before, but when they are interchanged, the corresponding names are interchanged as well.

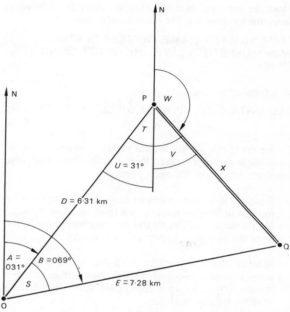

O: radar station   P, Q: aeroplane positions
W: aeroplane course bearing   ═══: aeroplane path

From a radar tracking station, an aeroplane is detected bearing 031° (bearing A), distance 6·31 km (distance D). Ten seconds later its bearing is 069° (bearing B), and distance is 7·28 km (distance E). Write a program to calculate the speed (in metres per second) and course bearing W of the aeroplane from this information. The calculation has the following steps:

1. Angle $S = B - A$
   $= 69 - 31 = 38°$

2. Calculate distance X from the cosine rule:
   $X^2 = D^2 + E^2 - 2DE \cos S$

3. Calculate angle T from the sine rule:
   $$\frac{\sin T}{E} = \frac{\sin S}{X}$$

4. Calculate angle V from $V = T - U$
   $= T - 31$

5. Calculate the bearing W from $W = 180 - V$

6. Calculate the speed from:
   speed $= X/10$ (m/s)

Note: Angles must be changed to radians when using sines and cosines, $180° = 3·14159$ radians.

125

Project program 5
Warehouse records

Records are kept at a warehouse, with the following information forming the file for each item:

ITEM NUMBER, NAME, NUMBER IN STOCK, MINIMUM STOCK LEVEL, RE-ORDER QUANTITY, PRICE

A typical data card would be:

106 DATA 4315, "POWER DRILL", 523, 100, 200, 14·76

Make up about 25 such data cards, and use them for the following operations. (It is probably easier to write separate programs for each section.)

1. Read an item number, and print all the information in the file for that item. Use a loop to work through all the data, reading all the information in each file, until the required item number is found.

   Modify this program to find the information for several items, reading all the files for each item required, and using a RESTORE statement before looking for the next item.

2. Read an item number, and a number of items added to the stock (or removed, using a negative quantity). Find the file for that item as in part 1, increase the number in stock by the number added, and print the contents of the file.

   Check if the number in stock is below the minimum stock level, in which case a suitable message is printed, including the cost of the number to be re-ordered.

3. Work out the total cost of all the items in stock. For each item:

   cost=number in stock × price

   and add up the total cost. Print a list with headings

   ITEM NO.   NAME   NO. IN STOCK   PRICE
                                        COST

   Remember that all the information must be read even if it is not all used.

Project program 6
Gas bills

The volume of gas that a person uses is recorded on his gas meter. Every three months this is read, the difference between the present and previous readings giving the volume of gas used. This volume is multiplied by the calorific value (the number of therms per cubic foot, usually about 500) to get the number of therms used. The cost is calculated as follows

fixed charge:	£1.25 per quarter
volume charges:	17.5p per therm for the first 100 therms
	12.98p per therm for the rest

(Preferably use current charges and calorific value for your area.)

For each of the customers, read:

	variables
account number	M
name	N$
address	A$
previous meter reading	R
date of previous reading	D$
present meter reading	P
date of present reading	E$

Calculate:

volume of gas used
=difference between the readings $V=P-R$

number of therms used
=volume × calorific value $H=V*C$

cost (see above)

Print an account, perhaps with this layout:

NAME: ...

ADDRESS: ......

	READINGS	DATE
PREVIOUS:	...	...
PRESENT:	...	...
VOLUME:	...	
THERMS:	...	
AMOUNT OWING: ...		

Project program 7
Motorway planning

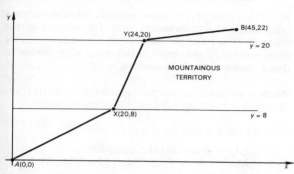

Towns A and B, 50 miles apart, are separated by a 12 mile wide belt of mountainous territory. A motorway is to be built joining the towns. It will cost £1 million per mile on normal ground, and £2 million per mile on mountainous territory. An approximate route is required which will make the total cost a minimum.

The positions of the towns, and the boundaries of the mountains are expressed in terms of co-ordinates. The route is divided into three straight sections, AX, XY and YB, where X and Y are points on the edges of the mountains. For various positions of X and Y, the distances AX, AY and YB are calculated, and the total cost of the motorway found. The positions of X and Y which give the minimum total cost are those through which a detailed route must be drawn.

Example

X at (20,8), Y at (24,20):

Distance AX

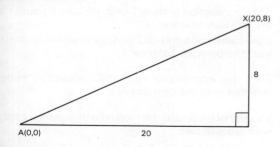

By Pythagoras's theorem:
$AX^2 = 20^2 + 8^2 = 464$
$AX = 21 \cdot 5$ miles

$\therefore$ Cost at £1m per mile $= £21 \cdot 5$ million

Distance XY

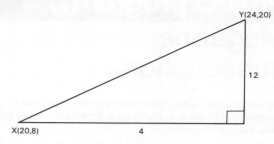

$XY^2 = 4^2 + 12^2 = 160$
$XY = 12 \cdot 6$ miles

$\therefore$ Cost at £2m per mile $= 12 \cdot 6 \times 2 = £25 \cdot 2$ million

Distance YB

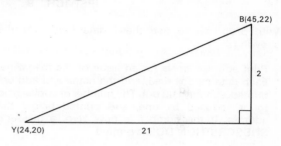

$YB^2 = 21^2 + 2^2 = 445$
$YB = 21 \cdot 1$ miles

$\therefore$ Cost at £1m per mile $= £21 \cdot 1$ million

Total cost $= £21 \cdot 5m + £25 \cdot 2m + £21 \cdot 1m$
$= £67 \cdot 8$ million.

Write a program which varies X and Y in a systematic way, calculating the total cost for each position, and obtains the positions giving the minimum cost.

The program must contain a variable recording the current minimum cost, and two others for the corresponding X and Y positions. As each new total cost is calculated, it is compared with this variable. If the new total is smaller, then the variable assumes its value, and the X and Y positions are noted. If it is larger, no action is taken. In this way, the minimum emerges from the program.

Project program 8
Magazine subscriptions

Records of the subscribers to a magazine are kept on a computer. For each subscriber, a data card shows the following information:

SUBSCRIBER NO., NAME, ADDRESS, NO. OF COPIES PAID FOR

For example:

109 DATA 19, "M. J. SMITH", "31 ELM WAY,
IPSWICH", 9

Write programs to use these data cards for the following:

1. Print address labels for an issue of the magazine. Each data card is read, and the name and address printed, suitably laid out. The number of copies paid for is reduced by one, and printed below the address. If the number is now zero, a message SUBSCRIPTION DUE is printed.

2. Record the payment of subscriptions. A card is read, containing a subscriber number and number of copies paid for. The subscriber cards are then read, until the corresponding subscriber number is found. The number of copies paid for is increased by the amount on the first card, and is printed, together with the subscriber's name and address.

Project program 9
Bank accounts

A bank account contains records of transactions (deposits and withdrawals) and the amount in the account (the balance) after each transaction. Every three months, a statement is prepared, with details of these transactions and balances.

Write a program to prepare statements for five accounts. For each account do the following steps:

1. Read the account header card, with

ACCOUNT NO., NAME, ADDRESS,
BALANCE FROM PREVIOUS STATEMENT

for example:

107 DATA 4173, "M. J. STUART", "41 LONG
LANE, NEWTON", 29·37

Print this information with the headings:

NAME: ACCOUNT NUMBER:
ADDRESS:
BALANCE CARRIED FORWARD:

DATE   TRANSACTION CODE   AMOUNT
                                BALANCE

2. Read a number of transaction cards, each with

DATE   TRANSACTION CODE   AMOUNT

The codes are:
1 deposit   3 interest added
2 withdrawal   4 bank charges

e.g.   216 DATA "30/8/76", 1, 47·63

Calculate the balance after each transaction:

if the transaction code is 1 or 3, add the amount to the previous balance

if the transaction code is 2 or 4, subtract the amount from the previous balance

Print the information from the transaction code together with the new balance.

3. The end of the account is marked with a marker card with amount zero:

e.g.   240 DATA "∗∗∗", 0, 0

When this card is read, a new account is started.

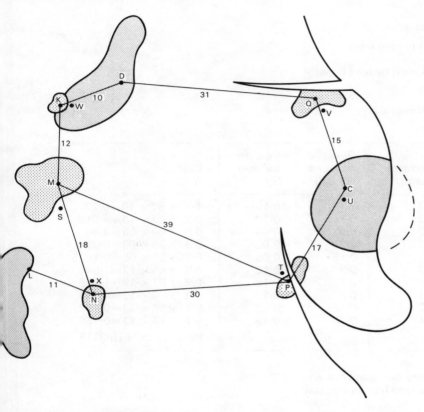

_____ : rail routes (distances in miles)
, M, N : industrial centres
, D : coal mines
: limestone quarry
, T, U, V, X, W : proposed steelworks sites

new steelworks is to be built at one of the following
tes:

: 4 miles from town M
: 2 miles from port P
: 1 mile from colliery C
: 3 miles from port Q
V : 1 mile from town K
: 2 miles from town N

he site selected will be the one where the rail transport
osts of the various raw materials and of the finished
roducts is a minimum.

he steelworks is to produce 1 million tons a year. The
w materials are as follows:

1·8 million tons of iron ore:
1·1 million tons imported at Q
0·7 million tons imported at P

0·8 million tons of coke:
0·5 million tons from C
0·3 million tons from D

0·15 millions tons of limestone from quarry at L.

The finished products will be distributed as follows:

0·3 million tons exported at P
0·2 million tons exported at Q
0·3 million tons sold at M
0·1 million tons sold at K
0·1 million tons sold at N

The transport costs are:

coal: £·08 per ton mile
limestone: £·05 per ton mile
iron ore: £·10 per ton mile
steel: £·12 per ton mile

Write a program to calculate the total rail transport costs of all the raw materials and of the finished product for each site. The site for which this total is the smallest will be chosen for the new steelworks.

The calculation works as follows:

For each item, the transport cost is:

cost = quantity × distance × cost per ton mile

For each site, a set of distances must be read from the map and used as input data.

The calculations (and suggested output layout) for site S are:

Item	Origin/ destin- ation	Distance (miles)	Quantity (millions of tons)	Cost per ton mile (£)	Cost (£m)
iron ore	from Q	57	1·1	0·10	1·1 ×57× ·10=6·27
iron ore	from P	43	0·7	0·10	0·7 ×43× ·10=3·01
coke	from C	60	0·5	0·08	0·5 ×60× ·08=2·40
coke	from D	26	0·3	0·08	0·3 ×26× ·08=0·624
limestone	from L	25	0·15	0·05	0·15×25× ·05=0·1875
steel	to P	43	0·3	0·12	0·3 ×43× ·12=1·548
steel	to Q	57	0·2	0·12	0·2 ×57× ·12=1·368
steel	to M	4	0·3	0·12	0·3 × 4× ·12=0·144
steel	to K	16	0·1	0·12	0·1 ×16× ·12=0·192
steel	to N	14	0·1	0·12	0·1 ×14× ·12=0·168
				total:	£15·9115

In the program, use lists to store the quantities and costs per ton mile. These are best read first, as they stay the same for all the sites.

For each site, read the distances, calculate the cost for each item, and the total cost. Print a table similar to the one above.

Project program 11
School records

Records are kept of the following information for each pupil at a school:

NAME   SEX   DATE OF BIRTH   YEAR
FORM   OPTION 1   OPTION 2 . . . OPTION 5

The options are the five optional subjects. They are coded as follows. Any subject may be in any option:

HI: history
GE: geography
ES: environmental studies
CS: computer studies
PH: physics
CH: chemistry
BI: biology
FR: French
WK: woodwork
MK: metalwork
DS: domestic science
AR: art

The form names are two letters for a member of staff.

A typical data card would be:

100 DATA "SMITH PAUL M.", "M", "21/03/62",
           4, "MR", "PH", "FR", "CH", "CS", "HI"

Use the following variable names:

N$: name   X$: sex   D$: date of birth
Y: year (ordinary variable)   F$: form

Use a list for the options:

P$(1): option 1
P$(2): option 2
. . .
P$(5): option 5

Make a list of this information for about 50 pupils, and use it for some of the following questions. In each case, read through all the information, and print the items required. RESTORE statements will be needed if the list is read more than once.

1. Print a list of the names and dates of birth of all the members of form MR.

   condition: is F$ = "MR"?

2. Print a list of the names, dates of birth and forms of all the members of the fourth year.

   condition: is Y=4?

3. Print a list of the names and forms of all the girls in the third year.

   conditions: is X$="F"?
               and Y=4?

4. Print a list of the names and forms of all the fifth year pupils doing biology as option 1.

   conditions: is Y =5?
               and P$(1)="BI"?

5. Print a list of the name, year and form of all the pupils doing art.

   conditions: is P$(1)="AR"?
               or P$(2)="AR"? etc.

   For each pupil, use a loop to work through the options.

6. Read the names of each form into a list G$(10) (if there are 10 forms). Use a loop to work through this list and, for each form, a nested loop to read all the information for the pupils. Print a list of the names and dates of birth of all the pupils in each form.

   condition: is G$(K)=F$?
                            K: form counter

Modifications

1. Adapt this program to suit the requirements of your own school.

2. Consider the advantages and disadvantages of such a system (preferably after you have the program running). Write an essay on your assessment of its value.

Project program 12
Standing in the queue

People arrive at a shop at an average rate of 2 per minute. The probability of a person arriving in any 1 second interval is $2/60 = 1/30$. The people are served one at a time, in the order of their arrival, again at an average rate of 2 per minute. The probability of a person leaving the shop in any 1 second interval is also $1/30$.

Write a program to keep a record of the number of people in the queue, using random numbers to determine whether a person arrives at the queue, or leaves the queue once every second, and printing the queue length once a minute. Read an initial queue length.

Method

Nested loops will be needed to count the number of minutes simulated (say 25), and the number of seconds for each minute.

To decide whether another person has arrived, a random number is taken. If it is less than $1/30$, then the queue length is increased by 1.

Similarly, another random number decides whether a person has finished being served. If this number is less than $1/30$, then the queue length is reduced by 1. If however the queue length is now negative, it is reset to zero.

At the end of each minute, print the number of minutes elapsed, and the length of the queue.

Modify the program to read different arrival and service probabilities, and to calculate the average queue length over the period simulated.

The ideas in this project are extended in Project Program 17: Simulating a road junction.

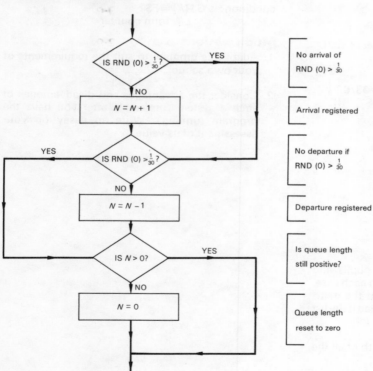

IS RND (0) $> \frac{1}{30}$? — YES — No arrival of RND (0) $> \frac{1}{30}$

NO

$N = N + 1$ — Arrival registered

IS RND (0) $> \frac{1}{30}$? — YES — No departure if RND (0) $> \frac{1}{30}$

NO

$N = N - 1$ — Departure registered

IS $N > 0$? — YES — Is queue length still positive?

NO

$N = 0$ — Queue length reset to zero

Project program 13
Population growth

The growth in the size of any population is proportional to its current size:

$$g = kp$$

p: size of population k: growth constant
g: growth of population in one year

For example, if the population is 50 million and the growth rate 2% ($k = \cdot 02$), then: $g = \cdot 02 \times 50 = 1$

The growth is 1 million.

The growth is added to the population size to get the size for the next year. In the example, the next year's population would be 51 million.

If the present size of the population of a country is known, together with its growth rate, its size for a number of future years can be calculated by using this method repeatedly.

Continuing the example:

Time (years)	Population (million)	Growth (million)
0	50	$\cdot 02 \times 50 = 1$
1	51	$\cdot 02 \times 51 = 1 \cdot 02$
2	52·02	$\cdot 02 \times 52 \cdot 02 = 1 \cdot 04$
etc.		

Write a program to carry out this calculation for a period of 25 years, reading an initial population and growth rate. Use figures from the table, or ones you have found out.

Country or region	Population (1970) (millions)	Growth rate (% per year)
Britain	56·0	0·5
USA	205·2	1·0
France	51·1	0·6
West Germany	58·6	0·6
India	554·6	2·6
China	759·6	1·8
USSR	242·6	1·0
Kuwait	0·7	8·3
Kenya	10·9	3·1
Peru	13·6	3·1
Africa	344·0	2·6
Asia	2056·0	2·3
North America	228·0	1·1
South America	283·0	2·9
Europe	462·0	0·8
Western Industrial States	705·0	1·01
Eastern Industrial States	369·0	0·96
Non-industrial states	2560·0	2·40
WORLD	3632·0	2·0

Note: A growth rate of 2·6% means the growth constant k in the formula is ·026.

Reference: John McHale, *World Facts and Trends*
(Collier)

Project program 14
The Solar System

The orbits of the planets around the Sun are approximately circular. Their radii, together with their times for a complete revolution, are listed below:

	Inner planets Orbital radius (million miles)	Period of revolution (days)
Mercury	36	86
Venus	67	225
Earth	93	365
Mars	142	687

	Outer planets Orbital radius (million miles)	Period of revolution (years)
Jupiter	483	12
Saturn	886	29
Uranus	1783	84
Neptune	2793	165
Pluto	3666	248

Write a program to read this information and do the following:

1. Calculate the circumference of the orbit

   $c = 2\pi r$

   $\pi = 3.14159$ r: orbit radius

2. For each planet, calculate the orbital speed in miles per hour.

   speed = circumference ÷ time of revolution (hours)

   (The revolution times must be changed to hours.)

3. Calculate the angle through which each inner planet has turned in three months (92 days)

   e.g.   Venus completes 360° in 225 days

   so in 92 days it does $\frac{92}{225} \times 360 = 147°$

4. Calculate the angle through which each outer planet has turned in one year.

Project program 15
Wage slips

Wage slips are prepared once a week for workers paid at an hourly rate. They contain information of hours worked, wages earned, tax, National Insurance contributions etc.

The input information required is:

	Use variable
Name	N$
Works number	W
Ordinary hours worked	H
Ordinary pay rate	R
Overtime hours worked	V
Overtime pay rate	S
Weekly tax-free allowance	A

The calculations are:

Gross pay = ordinary hours × ordinary rate + overtime hours × overtime rate $G = H \times R + V \times S$

Taxable pay = gross pay − tax free allowance $X = G - A$

Income tax = 35% of taxable pay $T = .35 \times X$

National Insurance contribution = 6% of taxable pay $I = .06 \times X$

Nett pay = gross pay − income tax − National Insurance contribution $P = G - T - I$

Write a program to read the input information for a number of workers (say 10), do the calculations, and print all the input and calculated information suitably set out as a wage slip. First read the date, and print it on each wage slip.

The calculation of income tax shown here is correct as long as the taxable pay is not more than £86. The complete calculations are done in Project Program 18.

Project program 16
Library records

A data card is prepared for each book in a library, containing the following information:

	Use variable
Author's surname	N$
Title	T$
Publisher	P$
Year of publication	D
Catalogue number (tells the subject)	C (from 0 to 1000)
Book number (identifies the book)	N

A typical data card would be:

200 DATA "WIENER", "THE HUMAN USE OF HUMAN BEINGS", "SPHERE BOOKS", 1968, 657·3, 15

Find out this information for 20 books. Write programs to use this information for the following questions. It is easier to write a separate program for each question.

1. Read the surname of an author, and then the book cards. Print a list of the title, date of publication and catalogue number of any books by that author.

2. Read a catalogue number, and then the book cards. Print a list of the author's surnames and titles of all the books having that catalogue number.

3. Read two catalogue numbers (smaller first), and then the book cards. Print a list of the authors' surnames and titles of all the books having catalogue numbers between the two read in.

4. Read a year, and then the book cards. Print a list of authors' surnames, titles and publishers of all the books published in that year.

5. Print the whole list of authors' names and titles in order of book number. Have a counter running from 1 to 20, and for each number read the list to find the book with that number.

Project program 17
Simulating a road junction

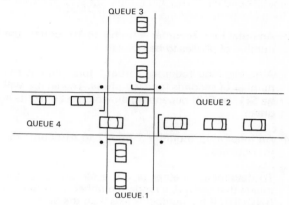

A road junction, as shown above, is controlled by traffic lights. To gain some idea of how it works, calculations are made once per second, to determine the number of cars in each of the four queues.

The lights are green for a number of seconds for queues 1 and 3, then green for a different number of seconds for queues 2 and 4. The orange phase is ignored in the simulation. When the lights are green, one car passes through the junction (and out of the queue) every second.

The probabilities of a car arriving at each of the queues in one second are read, together with the number of seconds green in each direction. The arrival probabilities should be between ·1 and ·7, averaging less than ·5, and the green times between 10 and 40 seconds. The object of the simulation is to find the green times which make the junction operate with as little delay as possible.

Use the following variables:

$N(4)$: number of cars in each queue (initial values can be input)

$P(4)$: probability of a car arriving during a 1 second interval in each queue (input)

$F(4)$: colour of lights in each direction: $+1$ for green, -1 for red (input the initial colours)

$S(2)$: number of seconds green in each direction (input), only values for queues 1 and 2 being needed.

The following program structure is suggested:

1. Read initial values of N, P, F and S.

   Print headings:

   NUMBER OF CARS IN QUEUE:

   TIME   QUEUE 1   QUEUE 2   QUEUE 3
                               QUEUE 4

2. An outer loop (counter A from 1 to 10) counts the number of phases to be simulated.

3. A middle loop (counter T from 1 to L) counts the number of seconds for each phase. The limit L will be $S(1)$ or $S(2)$ depending on which set of lights is green.

4. An inner loop (counter K from 1 to 4) counts the four queues.

   To determine whether or not a car arrives in the queue that second, a random number is taken (use RND(0)). If the number is less than the probability of arrival for that queue, then the queue length $N(K)$ is increased by 1.

   If the lights for that queue are green (if $F(K)=1$) the queue length $N(K)$ is reduced by 1. If it becomes negative, it is reset to zero. (A flow diagram of this section is in Project Program 12: Standing in the Queue.)

5. After the time loop, the phases must be altered and the time limit L changed. The phases are multiplied by -1, and the time limit changed as follows (change statement numbers for your program):

   105 IF L=S(1) THEN 120
   110 LET L=S(1)
   115 GO TO 125
   120 LET L=S(2)
   125 etc.

Modifications

1. Calculate the average length of each queue and the overall average.

   average queue length =

   $$\frac{\text{total of the queue lengths every second}}{\text{total number of seconds}}$$

2. Vary the times that each set of lights is green in order to minimize these averages.

Calculations of income tax are based on a person's total earnings over a year (called gross income).

A certain part of this income (the allowance) is tax free. The amount of the allowance depends on each person's circumstances. It is made up of the following items, where applicable:

Personal:	married man	£955
	single person or wife	£675
Children:	under 11	£240 per child
	11 to 15	£275 per child
	16 and over, till finished school	£305 per child
Dependent relative:	single woman claimant	£145 per relative
	other claimant	£100 per relative
Other:	housekeeper	£100
	blind person's allowance	£180

The allowances are deducted from a person's gross income to get that person's taxable income.

Example

Married man, two children under 11, gross income £4600.

Allowances:

personal	£955	gross income	£4600
children 2 × £240 =	£480	allowance	−£1435
total	£1435	taxable income	£3165

Income tax is paid at the following rates:

Basic: 35% of first £4500 of taxable income

Higher: 40% of next £500 of taxable income
45% of next £1000 of taxable income
50% of next £1000 of taxable income
55% of next £1000 of taxable income
60% of next £2000 of taxable income
65% of next £2000 of taxable income
70% of next £3000 of taxable income
75% of next £5000 of taxable income
83% of the rest.

Example

Taxable income £6700.

```
tax:  35% of  £4500  =  £1575
      40% of   £500  =   £200
      45% of  £1000  =   £450
      50% of   £700  =   £350
              £6700  total: £2575
```

The nett income is the amount after tax:

```
gross income:   £8200
tax:           −£2575
nett income:    £5625
```

Each person has a tax code, which is one tenth of their allowance (tax code 67 means allowance £670).

Write a program to read the gross income and tax code for a number of people, working out their taxable income, income tax and nett income.

Note: Every year, the figures used in this program change. Find out what the up-to-date figures are and use them in your program instead of the ones used here.

Project program 19
Installing central heating

If a house is to be heated to a constant temperature above its surroundings, heat will be lost from all the outside surfaces: ground floor, outer walls, windows, outside doors and roof. Heat will also be lost by ventilation—warm air from the inside will have to be exchanged for cold air from the outside. All the heat being lost must be continuously replaced by the central heating system. In order to determine the size of the central heating system, this rate of heat loss (measured in kilowatts) must be calculated.

Heat loss by conduction through surfaces

The heat loss through a surface depends on the nature of the surface, its area and the temperature difference from one side to the other.

heat loss (watts) = $U \times$ area (m²) × temperature difference (°C)

where U (watts per m² per °C) is a measure of the conductivity of the material. Required values of U are tabulated later.

Heat loss by ventilation

The rate of ventilation is measured by the number of air changes per hour. It requires 0·2 watts to heat one cubic metre of air 1 °C in one hour, so

heat loss (watts) = volume of air × number of air changes per hour × temperature difference (°C) × 0·2

The house is required to be heated to 20°C, with an outside temperature of −1 °C. All rooms are ventilated at one air change per hour.

Write a program to calculate the total heat loss from the house, using the following steps:

1. For the house design shown (or a design of your own), input the appropriate lengths and calculate the total area of: ground floor, walls, windows, doors, roof.

2. Using the appropriate U values, calculate the heat loss through each one.

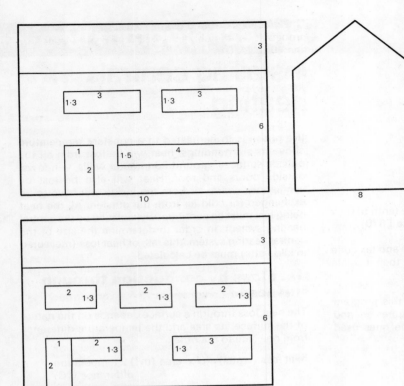

Example

Ground floor:

area = 10m × 8m = 80m²

heat loss = area × U × temperature difference
= 80 × 1·14 × 21 = 1850 watts

3. Calculate the volume of the house and hence the heat loss through ventilation at one air change per hour.

4. Calculate the total heat loss (and change from watts to kilowatts), which is the total heat requirement of the central heating system.

Table of U values

Surface	U (watts/m²/°C)
ground floor	1·14
cavity wall	1·93
window	5·68
door	2·41
tiled roof	3·32

Suggestions

1. Calculate the heat saved by insulating the walls and roof, and double glazing the windows. The appropriate U values are:

Insulated cavity walls:	0·48 (watts/m²/°C)
Insulated ceiling or roof:	0·90
Double glazed windows:	2·84

2. Run your program for different outside and inside temperatures.

Project program 20
Computer art

There are many ways to program a computer to print pictures. A simple method is suggested here, involving the use of random numbers.

A line printer page has 120 print positions in each line, and (about) 60 lines. The pictures are printed a line at a time, the list S$(120) storing the characters to be printed. The steps in producing the picture *reflections* are:

● The horizon is between lines 39 and 40. A loop counter Y works down the first 39 lines, while counter Z covers lines 40 to 60.

● The backgrounds use random numbers. The sky is either a space or a dot, with the probability of a dot going from 0 at the top to 1 at line 39.

To achieve this, a variable B has the value Y/39. (B is 1/39 in line 1 and 39/39=1 in line 39.) A counter works across the line (counter K from 1 to 120). For each character, a random number between 0 and 1 is compared with B (statement 35). If it is greater than B, the character is a blank. Otherwise the character is a dot.

The water background uses a similar method, with the probability of the character being a T going from 1 in line 40 to 1/20 in line 60.

● For the building, background characters are replaced by the letter M where necessary.

The building starts in line 25, so for earlier lines this part of the program is bypassed (the condition in statement 60). In the lines where the building occurs, it runs from column 76 to column 90. A loop is used (counter L from 76 to 90) to make these characters M's.

The reflection is printed in a similar way, except a random number is used to leave out some of the characters (statement 150).

● When all the characters in the list S$ have been filled in, a loop is used to print the line. This is done in statements 80 to 90 for lines above the horizon, and statements 165 to 175 for lines below it. In each case the program then moves on to a new line, starting again with the background.

Use this method, or a modification of it (or any other method), to inspire computer masterpieces of your own.

The program for the picture 'Reflections', shown below, is on the next page.

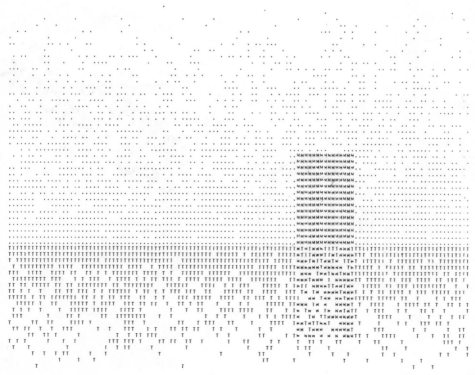

REFLECTIONS

Program

```
*TIME 300
2 PAGE
5 DIM S$(120)
10 READ A
15 LET B=RND(A)
20 FOR Y=1 TO 39
25 LET B=Y/39
30 FOR K=1 TO 120
35 IF RND(0)>B THEN 50
40 LET S$(K)="."
45 GO TO 55
50 LET S$(K)=" "
55 NEXT K
60 IF Y<25 THEN 80
65 FOR L=76 TO 90
70 LET S$(L)="M"
75 NEXT L
80 FOR M=1 TO 120
85 PRINT S$(M);
90 NEXT M
95 NEXT Y
100 FOR Z=40 TO 60
105 LET B=3-Z/20
110 FOR N=1 TO 120
115 IF RND(0)>B THEN 130
120 LET S$(N)="T"
125 GO TO 135
130 LET S$(N)=" "
135 NEXT N
140 IF Z>54 THEN 165
145 FOR P=76 TO 90
150 IF RND(0)>.6 THEN 160
155 LET S$(P)="W"
160 NEXT P
165 FOR R=1 TO 120
170 PRINT S$(R);
175 NEXT R
180 NEXT Z
182 PRINT "REFLECTIONS"
185 STOP
190 DATA 13
195 END
*
```